DOWN BOY

Joe Jerrett

Also by Joe Bennett

Just Walking the Dogs (Hazard Press)
Sleeping Dogs and Other Lies (Hazard Press)
Fun Run and Other Oxymorons (Scribner UK)
So Help Me Dog (Hazard Press)
Sit (Hazard Press)
Bedside Lovers (and Other Goats) (Scribner UK)
Doggone (Hazard Press)
Barking (Hazard Press)
A Land of Two Halves (Simon & Schuster UK)
Unmuzzled (Hazard Press)
Dogmatic (Hazard Press)

Down Boy

JOE BENNETT

HAZARD PRESS
publishers

The columns that make up this collection first appeared in the *Press*, the *Dominion Post*, the *Otago Daily Times*, the *Southland Times*, the *Waikato Daily Times*, *Hawke's Bay Today* and *New Zealand Gardener*.

Published by Hazard Press
P.O. Box 2151, Christchurch, New Zealand
www.hazardpress.com

First published 2006

ISBN 1-877393-25-8

Front cover photograph by Mike Bradstock
Cover design by Fiona Gartland, Hazard Press

Printed in New Zealand

Contents

For we are young and free

In the same week as the premier of New South Wales has taken steps to encourage Australian patriotism, Shane Warne, the well-known Australian cricketer, has agreed to take part in an episode of *Neighbours*, the well-known Australian drivel. What writer could resist the opportunity to submit a script for the show? Here's mine:

Establishing scene: a beach in the typically Australian town of Girt-by-Sea where typically Australian things are going on. Bush tucker is simmering in a billy on the Harvey Norman barbecue. A mass brawl on the beach is degenerating into a game of Aussie Rules. Surfers pass by en route to Paradise. They ignore a man in a safari suit shouting at crocodiles with bogus enthusiasm. At the high-tide mark, a Lebanese man lies groaning, a 40-ounce bottle of Bundaberg protruding at a decorative angle from his skull. Wholesome Australian girls in bikinis are using him as a beach volleyball net.

Cut to the inside of Matilda's condominium on Billabong Avenue. The doorbell rings. Matilda leaves off frying an emu's egg and waltzes to the door.

Shane Warne is standing on the step. His hair is gelled like a hedgehog. He is holding a toboggan in one hand and a CD case in the other.

Matilda waltzes two steps backwards with surprise, and one sideways.

Shane: Australians all, let us rejoice, for we are young and free.

Matilda: Mr Warne, what a lovely surprise. Been sledging, I see. But what brings you to the set of *Neighbours* where something dramatic happens in every episode, normally illustrating a point of contemporary concern such as racial tension or abortion or Aids, played for cheap emotion by a cast of young people who have been chosen for their sexiness rather than any ability to act?

Shane: Are you Matilda, headmistress of Girt-By-Sea Primary School?

Matilda: That's me, Mr Warne.

Shane: Well, in my capacity as Toohey's Light Patriotism Ambassador for the state of New South Wales, I bring you this. (*He hands her a CD in a green and gold case, etched with an exquisite image of original Australians in traditional tribal costume queuing at a liquor store.*) It's a recording of the national anthem which, by order of the state premier, you are to play at every Girt-By-Sea school assembly from now on, preferably with the children standing and singing along in joyful strains with one hand over their hearts and the other not up their noses.

Matilda: Crikey Dick, Mr Warne, our land may abound in nature's gifts of beauty rich and rare, such as red-back spiders, cane toads and chlamydia-riddled koalas, but don't you think we're getting a bit too much like the America of the South Pacific? Half our armed forces are in Iraq, we're becoming obese, we erect trade barriers on spurious grounds, and we export increasing numbers of tourists who have to shout to be heard above their clothes. So isn't a daily pledge of allegiance in schools just another step down Imitation-Yankee Avenue? Are you trying to come the raw prawn with me, Mr Warne, or some other equally incomprehensible local idiom?

Shane: How's that?

Matilda: Not out, but look who's coming.

Enter several pairs of speedos and miniature bikinis occupied by young Australian neighbours, leading a life of perpetual sunshine and complex coupling arrangements in order to titillate a global audience living in Speedo-and-bikini-less climes.

Shane stops a boy with blue hair.

Shane: What's your name, son?

Boy: Reddy.

Shane: Well, Reddy, are you a proud young Australian?

Reddy: Fair dinkum, Shane.

Shane: Good boy. And are you aware that, according to the premier of New South Wales, 'the national anthem is about community spirit, being a proud Australian and recognising our shared national identity'? And are you furthermore aware that from now on your schooling will include units on 'Australian Values'? And are you even furtherermore aware that our noble premier has defined these Australian values as family values, community harmony, national identity and other deeply meaningful abstract nouns? We've golden soil and wealth for toil and …

Matilda: Sorry to interrupt, Mr Warne – and I do deeply admire your efforts in the recent Ashes series, so tragically lost despite your venomous leg-breaks – but isn't this brain-washing? Isn't it the sort of platitudinous blather used throughout the ages to bolster the people in power, to induce uncritical allegiance, and ultimately to turn the young into potential war-fodder?

Shane: No.

Matilda. That's okay then. Right, kids, all together now, 'In joyful strains then let us sing'…oh no, look, a bush fire. We're all going to die. Run for it, young Australians, but don't stop singing.

Cut to credits, and nauseating theme music etc.

See me saw

There are tools, there are men's tools, and then there are chainsaws. A chainsaw is carnage on a stick. Whoever thought of the title *The Texas Chainsaw Massacre* could have stopped there. There was no need to make the film. Anyone could picture the pictures.

My neighbour is a manly man. He's got a chainsaw and I have coveted it. I have coveted it so hard I couldn't sleep. I watched him fell a tree last week. Brrrm, brrrm, yeeaow, crack, shudder, topple, BOOM. I find it hard to imagine a more manly sentence than that.

Having chopped the tree down the neighbour then chopped it up. Some time in the future the bits will turn into smoke and heat. Heat for nothing. I wanted free heat too.

My previous house had a gas fire. The gas came in chemistry-lab cylinders at $70 a pop which I didn't mind paying because I had no alternative. But my new house came with a log burner and I resented paying for wood. Wood is everywhere. The stuff grows on trees. I took to collecting driftwood from the beach and twigs from dog walks. But in the evening as I huddled round my twig heap I imagined my neighbour standing like an eighteenth-century squire with his back to a monstrous hearth, spreading his tailcoat to toast his buttocks, and I felt envy.

The solution to envy lay in the steep paddock behind my house where several trees had been felled and forgotten by the previous owner. Those trees were heat for the taking, heat for nothing.

Of the two assistants in the chainsaw shop, one was old and one young. When I stepped through the door they both recognised my manliness on the instant and raced to be first to make its acquaintance. The younger won at a canter.

'I want a chainsaw,' I said, because that's how manly men talk. Terse, spare, emphatic.

'Good,' he said.

'Yes,' I said.

'What size?' he said.

'Big,' I said.

'Right,' he said and he rubbed his hands together in the universal sawyer's gesture indicating free warmth to come.

The chainsaw cost $1800. Protective chaps cost $200, steel-tipped boots $100, safety glasses $25, safety helmet $25 and banana-coloured ear muffs $20. The assistant also wanted to charge me $10 for a petrol can but I raised a manly eyebrow and he threw the can in for free. Most men just shop, you see, but manly men cut deals.

The chainsaw had a 25-inch bar. I liked that. Imperial measurements are manly. When I got the thing home the dogs barked at it. 'Good dogs,' I said, and donned my safety gear.

If you've ever carried a big chainsaw up a steep paddock wearing steel-tipped boots, helmet, glasses, ear muffs, a manly expression and a pair of chaps that seem to be made out of carpet, you'll know that it's warm work. You may also know that it's warm work walking back down a steep paddock to fetch the instruction manual.

The manual kicked off with forty-eight pages of safety instructions all of which I skipped apart from an amusing paragraph about the perils of white finger. Then page forty-nine explained that starting the engine was a simple business of depressing the compression valve, engaging the chain brake, squeezing the throttle trigger, adjusting the cotter pin spindle, calibrating the carburettor sprocket, then setting a steel-tipped toe into the handle of the chainsaw and tweaking the starter rope. And sure enough the mighty beast roared into life before you could say 'two pauses to demist the safety glasses and a mental note to self to ring the chiropractor'.

Stripping a trunk of branches proved entertaining. The chainsaw tended to seek out branches I wasn't aiming at. Then it would leap and roar like a stallion. 'Whoa,' I'd bellow in a manly voice, hoping that the neighbour would emerge to admire me. He didn't but it didn't matter. After little more than an hour I had stripped two yards of trunk. After that it was like slicing a giant salami. The engine roared, sawdust flew and a round dropped, neat as a hockey puck. I cut eight rounds then stilled the engine, laid the saw aside and just stood there, dripping sweat, sprayed with sawdust, my steel-tipped boots planted firmly on my own soil as the sun sank in the west. At my feet a pile of logs. In my heart a primitive satisfaction. I kicked a log. It rolled, gathered momentum, bounced like a tennis ball, cleared the fence, astonished a dog and crashed into the tin wall of the woodshed. The boom echoed round the valley and I felt good.

The logs lasted the whole evening.

Not if, but when

'It's not if,' said a virologist, 'but when.' With that one simple sentence he condemned a nation to its fate. He strapped New Zealand to the railway track as the H5N1 Express bore down en route from Media to Public. The train had no brakes. The track had no points. The metal wheels had no pity. The result was horrible to behold. New Zealand suffered an appalling case of fear of bird flu.

Symptoms vary. According to phobologists, the most obvious sign that the disease has taken hold is a slight but measurable distension of the vocabulary. The words 'virus', 'mutate' and especially 'pandemic' stream from the victim's mouth, along with entire phrases such as 'cross the species barrier'. Such phrases are known to phobologists as 'lexical floaters'. Though they appear to be associated with intellectual substance, closer examination, even under an ordinary household magnifying glass, reveals that they are attached to no scientific knowledge whatsoever.

Phobologists are at pains to remind the public that lexical floaters are extraordinarily contagious and that once contracted they are terminal. Any amateur examination should be conducted in ear muffs.

The fear virus works, say experts, by attaching itself to pre-existing fear radicals, left over from past fear epidemics. Capable of lying dormant for years, these radicals respond instantly to gossip or newspaper articles. They are particularly sensitive to television images, especially if these show scientists in white coats filling test tubes from a multiple glass pipette like a horse comb. Energised by these images, fear radicals will attach themselves automatically to the nearest jargon.

Like all fear viruses, the fear-of-bird-flu virus also contains a memory-killer gene. It supplants and suppresses all memories of fear of SARS, Ebola, Y2K, fat, global warming, tsunami, crime, coffee, cholesterol, earthquakes, paedophilia, the sun, snakes, house price collapse, asteroids, terrorism, rising sea level, butter, spitting, dogs and tap water.

At the same time the virus attacks the part of the brain responsible for reasoning. The skill of drawing conclusions from historical evidence is entirely disabled. Without it the brain cannot discern that previous fears have come to nothing, or that fear of the unknown is usually worse than the unknown when it finally makes itself known.

The effects are immediate. Stockpiling is a common response, as is a sense that the human being is a doomed beast in a hostile world. This can lead to lassitude, depression and fatalism, or to a frantic burst of activity characterised by bunker building or even credit-card binging.

The most extreme symptom appears comical at first but requires immediate hospitalisation. Belief in and prayer to a supreme being who is benign and yet simultaneously responsible for bird flu, is so severe a case of mental inconsistency that it must be treated within moments of infection if the patient is to have any hope of recovery.

Leading phobologists are at odds over the efficacy of vaccines against fear of bird flu. The makers of one popular vaccine acknowledged that they were uncertain whether their product offered anything other than temporary relief. 'But in the midst of a pandemic such as this one,' said a spokesman for Scottish Distilleries, 'surely any relief is better than none. Our vaccine promises at least one evening free from the fear virus before the end of the world arrives the next morning. Ours is also an ideal vaccine to stockpile. It works in the same temporary way against all known fear viruses, and it improves with age.'

Phobologists and government bodies generally prefer a vaccine known as Tammy-CD. Governments have drawn on vast stockpiles of Tammy-CD to immunise front-line workers such as experts and newsreaders. The active agent in Tammy-CD is the upbeat music of Tammy Wynette, the Country and Implant star. Tammy-CD is believed to work by causing the brain to secrete massive quantities of cheap sentiment, thereby depriving the fear virus of attention and causing it to shrivel.

Experts are united, however, in condemning one common form of treatment. 'The serious news item,' said a leading phobologist, 'suggesting that there is no need to panic, that bird flu may well arrive but there's nothing much anyone can do to stop it and certainly no point in worrying about it before it arrives, and that it will probably prove less deadly than the motor cars that we love, is laughable. By denying the need for panic such an item only adds to that panic.' For evidence he directed reporters to a research paper in a recent issue of *Phobology Quarterly*, entitled 'The Pathology of Panic – or the Corporal Jones Syndrome'.

'In short,' he went on, 'it's too late. The fear of bird flu has now escaped into the general population and there is nothing to do but to let it run its course. Eventually it will peak and be replaced by another fear. Or, of course, by bird flu, which would be a relief.'

Joe, you're an angel

Before last weekend I had attended only one surprise party. When the captain of the lowly rugby team I played for turned forty, an old friend took him to the pub. Meanwhile everyone else he'd ever known descended on his house, hid in the basement and turned out the light.

When the birthday boy came home his wife played the fishwife. We heard it all through the floor. Who did he think he was, buggering off to get drunk when they were supposed to be going out to dinner? She let fly with plenty of the words that journalists render with asterisks. It was a superb performance, though, to be frank, it sounded as though she might have done it before. Finally she sent him down to the basement on a spurious errand.

He opened the door, turned on the light and found himself confronted by every face he knew in the world. For a moment he just stared. Then we burst into 'Happy Birthday' and he burst into tears. He was not the sort of man who is easily given to tears. It was a fine moment.

So when last week a friend proposed a surprise party for his wife's birthday I said it was a splendid idea and what time should we all arrive.

'That's up to you,' he said.

'Eh?' I said.

'You see,' he said, 'it's impossible to keep anything from my wife, so I was wondering whether perhaps, Joe, you might be willing, as a favour, and I'll be in your debt for ever, to have the party at, um, well, you know, your place.'

'My place?'

'Your place.'

Time was when the word party beckoned irresistibly. It sang with excitement and whispered of sex.

Sex rarely attended the same parties I did, but that didn't stop it whispering. And even without sex there were the joys of disinhibition and of watching other people fight.

But not any more. At forty-eight I am now so set in my inhibitions that they have become the whole of me. At the same time the whisper of sex and the bellow of booze have been drowned by the siren song of cocoa and an early night.

As for having a party at my place, well, it was unthinkable. I'd have to clean the toilet. I'd have to stay up right to the end with the sort of people who treat parties in the same way as limpets treat rocks. At four in the morning they'd want to moan about their relationships before rummaging through my bathroom for razor blades. And since it wouldn't actually be my party I wouldn't even know the names of the people who were breaking my furniture, missing the toilet bowl, throwing up in my garden, de-alphabetising my books, leaving glasses of dog-ends beneath my chairs, ransacking my booze cabinet late at night in search of something vivid to make cocktails with, sneaking into my spare bedroom and wedging the door shut with my bookshelves in order to have sex without letting me watch, then crashing on my sofa and farting through the night and being there in the morning to eat my bacon, my eggs and my aspirins. It was out of the question.

'Good idea,' I said. 'Let's have the party at my place.'

'Really?' he said.

'Yes, really,' I said.

'Joe,' he said, 'you're an angel.' Which was nice of him but wrong. I wasn't an angel. I didn't want to host the party. But I did want to seem to want to host the party. I wanted to seem like the sort of generous and uninhibited bloke who spontaneously lends his house to other people to hold parties in. If I'd said no I would have showed myself to be mean and cautious and inhibited and selfish.

As Saturday approached I increasingly cursed myself for having agreed to hold the party, which proved only that I was mean and cautious and inhibited and selfish, a catalogue of adjectives to which I had now added dissembling and hypocritical. But it was too late to back out.

On the big night my task was to collect the birthday girl, take her for a walk with my dogs and then drive her back to my house on the pretext that I'd forgotten her present. In the meantime every one of her multiple relatives, friends and colleagues would have hidden in my lounge and turned off the lights.

When we drove up to my house it seemed impressively deserted. If there were cars I couldn't see them. If there were people I couldn't hear them. I sent the birthday girl upstairs to find her present while I turned the car round. I pictured her walking into the darkened room, turning on the light and screaming.

The scream came bang on cue. By the time I got upstairs she was sipping brandy and merely crying. 'You bastard,' she said when she saw me, which was flattering.

It proved a very middle-aged party. Nothing got broken, everyone thanked me, and by one in the morning they'd all gone home to cocoa. Hubby then spent the next day scrubbing my house to a cleanliness it had never before achieved, and telling me what a top-notch chap I was. And now, three days later, I almost believe I'm the sort of bloke he thinks I am.

Funny and true

What a coup for cartooning. I have heard it suggested that a dozen cartoons, from Denmark of all places, may yet spark World War III. They won't, of course, because the leaders of Islam know they haven't got enough guns, but it's nice to know that the art of caricature still packs a kick.

The purpose of a cartoon is not to be funny. Being funny is the method. The purpose of a cartoon is to tell the truth. Truth is immediately recognisable and often funny.

The Muslim world has not found the cartoons funny. The ostensible reason is that Islam forbids pictures of Mohammed. But that reason doesn't stand up to scrutiny. Five minutes on the Internet and I had discovered several pictures of Mohammed. I am also reliably informed that you can buy a picture of Mohammed in the central market at Teheran. So, there must be something else that's upsetting the Islamic world to the point that they're firebombing embassies, marching down Queen Street and boycotting Danish yoghurt.

I have seen only two of the cartoons. The first depicts Mohammed with a bomb in his turban. It is not particularly witty. The point it is obviously making is that some people commit acts of murder in the name of the prophet. Equally obviously, that point is true.

The reaction of a few Muslims has been funnier than the cartoon. 'Slay those who insult Islam,' said one placard carried by a protester, thereby exquisitely reinforcing the point of the cartoon he is protesting against. He reminds me of the Christian fundamentalist who murdered an abortionist on the grounds that the abortionist committed murder.

The second cartoon is wittier. It depicts Mohammed emerging from Muslim heaven to apologise to a stream of dead suicide bombers for having run out of virgins. The reference is to the promise of 144 virgins to anyone who dies for the Islamic cause. (What attitude this implies to women, I shall ignore for the moment, though it does make me wonder what female suicide bombers get in the hereafter. A gross of Islamic Brad Pitts? A platinum burka?)

What has been ignored amid the eruption of belligerence, apology, and yoghurt-flinging is that the two cartoons invite two simple questions: First, does Islam condone suicide bombers? Does it approve of people blowing themselves up and killing the innocent? If so, then cartoons should be only the start of the mockery. Such a faith should be as universally condemned as Nazism. If not, if Islam does not approve of murder, then every imam and ayatollah should stand up and say so.

Second, is it a tenet of the Islamic faith that suicide bombers get a gross of virgins in heaven? If so, then once again the faith should be universally condemned. If not, then every imam and ayatollah should stand up and say so. And if they did, the hated cartoons would stop.

What has prevented these simple questions being asked is the usual argument about respect. It is our duty, the argument runs, to respect other people's beliefs. I, for one, have never had any idea why. Anything true can always withstand mockery. Copernicus's belief that the earth moved round the sun endured everything the Catholic Inquisition could throw at it. And the Inquisition didn't just print cartoons. It pulled out fingernails. It incinerated its enemies. But the truth endured.

Moreover, the rule about respecting other religions is selectively maintained. If a religion is small it is known as a cult, and a cult is fair game. But the established religions are all former cults. They just happened to get big. Their beliefs are every bit as wacky as the beliefs of little cults. Not questioning those beliefs is not an act of respect. It's merely not upsetting the status quo.

The Western belief that has sparked this controversy is the belief in freedom of speech. It's a belief I share, because history demonstrates that a free press is our best defence against tyranny. Every tyrant in history has muzzled the press.

Ostensibly our leaders share my belief, but when the heat came on they renounced it.

'I approve of freedom of the press,' said Helen Clark on television, 'but…'

'I approve of freedom of the press,' said Don Brash on television, 'but…'

In other words, both of them worried more about votes or exports than about the truth.

In doing so they echoed Hamdi Hassan, an Egyptian MP. 'Freedom of expression,' said Mr Hassan, 'does not mean people are free to insult prophets.'

I'm sorry, Mr Hassan, but that is precisely what it does mean. Freedom means freedom. And if a prophet is really a prophet he's not going to get upset.

The vast majority of the one and a half billion Muslims in this world are good and peaceable people. They don't blow themselves up. They don't hate the West. They are superb hosts. They love their children. They are closer to Mohammed than their leaders are. The same is true of Christians and Christ.

Each religion began with one man. Both men were apparently tolerant. Each man proposed a system of living, a code of social behaviour. After their deaths, however, those teachings became perverted. They became dressed in nonsensical theology. That theology ossified into a system for gaining and retaining power. It became, in other words, merely political. The grip of the Islamic authorities in Iran is indistinguishable from the grip of, say, the Catholic authorities in Spain and Ireland well into the twentieth century, or the grip of the Communist Party in the Soviet Union. Such a grip is a noxious thing.

And if a dozen cartoons can shake it, it's a vulnerable thing.

In the name of the people

MMP has turned election night into a variety show. You never know what you're going to get and you have to wait a long time for the main acts. In the end I enjoyed the support acts more.

Nandor Tanczos didn't get back into parliament but he did turn up at TVNZ for a chat. He wore his hair in a bun. It sat on his head like a coil of rope on the wharf. With his professorial glasses he looked exactly like one of those radical Muslim clerics on an Aljazeera videotape.

I feel sorry for Nandor. Not because he lost his seat but because he's condemned himself to perpetual adolescence. How will he manage the descent into age and sense? When he thins on top will he retain a couple of metres on the side? Will he collect his pension by skateboard?

I didn't feel sorry for Peter Dunne, even though he wanted me to. He was indignant that TVNZ had ignored him. Once he was certain that he'd got two mates into parliament on the back of getting himself into parliament he emerged to meet the flashlights. Flashlights are never kind to Mr Dunne. He looked like an indignant piglet with kiss curls. He tried very hard to seem full of gravitas but it emerged as pique. What he ignored is that he was ignored because he's so ignorable.

Rodney Hide looked more than ever like Humpty Dumpty. If you pushed him over on Queen Street he'd keep rolling. What Humpty knew but didn't say was that the people who voted for him weren't really voting for him. He read a prepared script that was as thrilling as Peter Dunne.

The Maori Party had a lot of fun. They ate, drank, sang and waved flags. Pita Sharples showed off a magnificent set of teeth. Auntie Tariana glided around like a Dalek on Prozac. She held a superbly phoney cellphone call with the smoulderingly happy Hone Harawira. The main topic of conversation was their respective mokopuna. One of those mokopuna had earlier appeared wearing a cowboy hat, but she had been sent away to take it off in case she was mistaken for Dover Samuels. Meanwhile Dover Samuels lost and made a speech that demonstrated why.

Commentators stumbled all night over the Maori language. On TV3 John Campbell made Te Tai Hauauru sound like a wolf addressing the moon. No one corrected him. Indeed a Maori reporter congratulated him on his pronunciation. She pronounced pronunciation pronounciation. No one corrected her either. Every Maori interview began with a bicultural kia ora then gave up.

Don Brash looked less like Dr Death than he had for a month. Perhaps he was relieved to have lost creditably. At least now he wouldn't have to try to abolish a Maori seat that Pita Sharples was sitting on. In an all-in brawl you wouldn't have fancied Don's chances. Nor in a tag match would you have backed John Key against Hone Harawira. And as for when the Dalek came off the Prozac – no, they were better off out of it.

But the Nats had recruited at least one street fighter. Bob the Builder Clarkson looked willing to pick a fight with anyone. Could he fix the gnome of Tauranga? Yes he could. Winston had asked the electorate to judge him on his record and they had.

When Winston learned that he had still snuck through the back door because 5 per cent of the population suffered from blue rinses and memory loss, he tried to switch the lighthouse grin back on. But it was unconvincing. Pita Sharples out-toothed him by several hundred watts.

Helen finally arrived in the high-collared red outfit that makes her look like an off-duty hussar. It is always a shock to see Helen's teeth after six weeks of billboards. She handed her flowers to her husband and said, 'Thank you, mainstream New Zealand,' to the 40 per cent of New Zealanders who voted for her. It was the only dig she allowed herself. She said she felt humbled. Several other winners had already said they felt humbled. None of them had looked humbled. Nor did Helen.

But she then dropped her voice an octave and did gravitas a lot better than Peter Dunne. She said she wanted to heal the divisions between mainstream New Zealand and the nasty filthy capitalist greedmongers who had the big money. She was willing to talk to anyone and everyone except the nasty filthy capitalist greedmongers who had captured 40 per cent of the non-mainstream vote.

The camera cut to Peter Dunne, to Gnome Central, to a littered marae and to Green Party HQ, where Jeanette Fitzsimons was standing next to Mr Fitzsimons. He looked like Jebediah the Amish.

This variety show could run for weeks.

Dead classy

Class is bad. We sneer at class. We've been taught to. Class is suppression. Class is just a system for keeping power in the hands of the few and impotence in the lives of the many. Or so goes the contemporary wisdom. And, like most contemporary wisdom, it's far from the whole truth.

Power is always in the hands of the few. If it weren't, it wouldn't be power. The revolutionary expression 'power to the people' makes as much sense as a speech by Mr Peters. And everyone who acquires power in the name of the people ends up dead, swinging by the ankle from a lamppost but still clutching the title deeds to a fleet of aeroplanes and a holiday home in Antibes with ensuite bullion.

Every society has a system of class. The notion that Soviet Russia didn't was an obvious myth, as is the notion that New Zealand doesn't. Just take a walk down the main street now and look. The system of class is less entrenched here than in some places but it is emphatically there.

For any system of class to endure it has to be a little squidgy. It must be possible for a citizen to shift between classes. If the system is squidgeless it becomes ossified and then it shatters. Having shattered, it is always rebuilt. The difference between the old system and the rebuilt one is nugatory.

Class has something to do with money, but it should have something to do with something else. For the word class carries a secondary meaning. If we describe someone as a classy cricketer, it means he plays with an ease and elegance, an apparent disdain for unseemly striving. And so it is with social class. For an upper class to be truly upper it must deport itself in a better way than the masses do. It must take the long view. It must rise above sentiment and simple urges. It must have dignity. It must have, like a duvet, loft. Of course it normally doesn't. True class is rare. But when it does occur, and it can occur anywhere, it's delicious and it's admirable.

Here's a story of class. An old English woman sent it to me recently. She was there. She saw it happen. It was a birthday party.

The old boy whose birthday was being celebrated was turning seventy, three score and ten, the full allotted span beyond which anything is a bonus. He was a distinguished chap in some field or other. His wife was a doctor. She threw the party. She had a surprise present for him. That present was a newly commissioned musical setting of one of Shakespeare's sonnets.

Now, if you're thinking, Oh dear, then I'm with you. I've heard a few musical settings of poetry in my time and I wouldn't want to sit through any of them again. But no one gets everything right.

Of Shakey's 154 sonnets, the undeservedly best known is 'Shall I compare thee to a summer's day?' Mrs Wifely Doctor didn't choose that one. She chose the second best-known and a far better poem. 'When in disgrace with fortune and men's eyes,' it begins, 'I all alone beweep my outcast state.'

She hid a chamber orchestra and a la-di-da tenor behind a curtain before the guests arrived. Then came a couple of hours of eating and drinking and subdued elderly merriment. Eventually a botrytised whatever was served, with coffee and petits fours, the tables were cleared, Mrs Wifely Doctor tapped a spoon against faultless crystal and silence spread like a nice contagion. Birthday Boy stood to speak.

He thanked everyone for coming. He made a little self-abasing joke. And then he faltered. 'I feel a little unwell,' he said. 'I think I'd better sit down.' He smiled a reassuring apology as he spoke, and according to my correspondent he didn't look too bad. Just a bit groggy, she thought, a little woozy with wine and excitement.

He sat down beside his wife on a chair of red plush with ornate gilt mouldings, slumped forward and died. His head hit the table, though without making much of a bang. The hall was silent. Mrs Wifely Doctor felt his pulse. She kissed the top of his head. Then she stood and announced that he was dead and she asked everyone to please stay. She went and came back with four waiters. Under her directions they carried her husband out of the hall on his chair. She returned quite soon.

'This is my present to my husband,' she announced, and the curtain peeled back to reveal the chamber orchestra and the la-di-da tenor who duly delivered the first public performance of an original setting of 'When in disgrace with fortune and men's eyes'.

Now that's class.

Badlands revisited

The lure of Cliché-Land is as persistent as herpes, and Pete and I were itching to go again.

On previous visits we'd toured the merry city of Winwin Situation and we'd trudged through the rubble of Worst Case Scenario. But still we itched to see for ourselves the fabled land of sporting metaphor, known to travellers as Totally Awesome City.

We needed a guide. At the local guide market only the Time family was available for hire. Young Son Time would wait for no man, so we engaged Old Father Time, half brother to Ole Man River, in the hope that he would just keep rolling and not say nothing except double negatives. We loaded him into the canoe along with his scythe and a fishing rod and set out for the dangerous waters of Cliché.

After a day of paddling we beached the canoe. While Time made a fire I cast my fishing line, hauled up a red herring and offered it to Time, but he had other fish to fry. 'Look over there,' he said. On a barren beach on Cliché Island an assortment of creatures lounged, seemingly inert.

'Tired expressions, I presume,' I said.

''Fraid not,' said Time. 'Those are accidents.'

'Accidents? But they look fine.'

‘They’re waiting to happen,’ said Time. ‘Watch.’

He drew himself up to his full four foot six. Time was short. ‘Yoohoo,’ he bellowed. The creatures looked up. ‘Your Time has come.’

The effect was dramatic. All around us the accidents suddenly happened. Bang. Crash. Glass shattered. Limbs flew. A cylindrical metal accident flung itself from a wall, split open at my feet and disgorged a mass of slimy limbless creatures. Directly above Pete’s head a second cylinder prepared to jump.

‘Look out,’ I screamed, ‘another can of worms.’

Pete dived for safety.

‘Let’s get out of here,’ I said.

He nodded sagely, then onionly. Pete was a seasoned traveller.

‘It’s not as easy as it looks,’ said Time. ‘This is the dreaded valley of Mixed Animal Metaphors.’

‘I smell a rat,’ sniffed Pete. But before he could smell it again a giant fowl made of coiled metal nipped the rat in the bud.

‘I know what you’re thinking,’ said Time, ‘but that was no spring chicken. Look yonder.’ Behind the rat’s corpse a stream of previously unnoticed bony figures were rising from previously unnoticed furniture.

‘Oh no,’ I said, ‘the skeletons in the cupboard.’

‘Yes,’ said Time, ‘and they’re coming home to roost. Duck!’

The duck flew past but the skeletons swooped towards the canoe. I tossed them the red herring, then seized the initiative and paddled with it. Pete tried to wrest the initiative from me but I seized a window of opportunity and he paddled with that. Time seized the day and together we paddled madly away.

We paddled for an hour without stopping. We paddled past the Island of Travel Advertising Cliché where locals danced in native costume and a perfect couple bathed in a limpid lagoon then dined at sunset beneath a swaying coconut palm. It was so stultifyingly predictable that the three of us sank dangerously towards coma. But at that moment an aged rock star fell from the coconut palm and killed the dancers, the perfect couple and himself, so we all cheered up. On we paddled past Economic Cliché Land where interest rates spiralled decoratively round the Mountains of Debt. At one stage we passed through the perilous Territory of Real Estate Clichés, but we knew to keep our eyes averted. One glimpse and our indoor-outdoor flow would cease for ever.

'Stop paddling,' said Time suddenly. He stood up and trod on our fingers.

'What the…?' exclaimed Pete, but we had Time on our hands.

'I think we're there,' said Time, pointing. Following his finger we saw back gardens running down to the water's edge. Time biffed his scythe. It landed with a clatter and bounced.

'Yep,' said Time, 'behold Totally Awesome City with its famous hard yards.'

We disembarked cautiously. On the horizon hung a threatening injury cloud, but the Isle of Sporting Metaphor was eerily quiet. We passed through a manicured park where stood eight giant balls of rock. A strange shape lounged among them.

'Just a ball park figure,' said Time. 'Ignore him.'

Beyond the last of the eight balls we approached a little wicket gate. Just then we heard a rumbling growl below and behind us.

'Oh no,' said Time, 'the cellar-dwellers. Run.'

We sprinted for the wicket gate. Pete won the race by a short head and rammed the gate with it. His short head stuck fast to the palings. I ran to help him but I stuck to the gate even faster.

Time stood still. I held my breath, lost my grip and held Pete's breath instead. The rumbling of cellar-dwellers drew nearer.

From out of the shadows sidled the ball park figure.

'Gentlemen,' it said, its face a wicked leer, 'I think it would be fair to say that you're behind the eight ball.'

'And on a very sticky wicket,' added Pete, grimly.

Pam's pups

The dictionary defines sentiment as mawkish tenderness. I would define it as the impulse that causes women of a certain age to lean into a pram, say coochy-coo, plant a leathery kiss and give the pram's occupant its first acquaintance with terror.

The subject of sentiment arises because of the events of last weekend. On Saturday morning I discovered that I suddenly had nine extra mouths to feed, and on Sunday morning I discovered Pamela Anderson. Ms Anderson was on the front page of the paper. She was standing between two Royal Canadian Mounted Policemen and behind a similar number of breasts. Each policeman was about the size of an adult fur seal. Each breast was about the size of a fur seal pup.

The comparison is deliberate because Ms Anderson is concerned about fur seal pups. Every year the fishermen of Canada club several thousand fur seal pups to death, and Ms Anderson, along with other luminaries such as Brigitte Bardot and Sir Paul and Lady McCartney, would like to stop them doing so. To this end Ms Anderson has flung the weight of her breasts behind the anti-cull campaign, which should give it significant momentum.

The reason that Ms Anderson is concerned about fur seals cannot be that the species is threatened, because it isn't. The Canadian fur seal population has grown considerably over the last thirty years. No, what Ms Anderson objects to is simply the fact of the innocents being clubbed.

Now, I'm confident Ms Anderson does not object to infant flies being sprayed to death, nor to baby rats being poisoned to death, and I am equally confident that if Ms Anderson were to find a preschooler snake in her bedroom and I were to happen to be passing by and hear her cries of horror and charge heroically into her bedroom and club the thing into the hereafter, Ms Anderson's gratitude would be so all-embracing that I would be threatened with asphyxia. But flies, rats and snakes, of course, are not seal pups. Seal pups have Bambi eyelashes, eyes like saucers and snub little noses. In short they look like human babies. By looking so cute they arouse the soft emotions that mosquito larvae, for example, are utterly incapable of arousing in anyone but Mr and Mrs Mosquito. In other words, Pamela Anderson is being sentimental.

You'll be surprised to learn that I have never clubbed a snake to death in Ms Anderson's bedroom, nor even visited her house, and neither has Ms Anderson visited mine. And I am particularly glad that she didn't pay an inaugural visit a couple of weeks ago because I was doing my best to imitate the Canadian fishermen. I was trying to perform a pre-emptive cull.

I keep chooks. I also keep a rooster. The rooster has achieved a way of life that many men aspire to. He eats, does no work, makes a lot of noise and has sex twenty times a day. Were it not for the sex he could be mistaken for certain members of parliament.

But because of the sex, every egg that is laid on my section is a potential chook. I don't want more chooks and I emphatically don't want more roosters. I try, therefore, to intercept and eat all the eggs, but for obvious evolutionary reasons hens are fond of hiding them. And when a hen of mine disappeared for several days I presumed that she had managed to stash a clutch of eggs and was planning to turn them into a pramful of chooks and roosters. In a bid to thwart her I packed a club and a few essentials in a haversack and set out with the dogs on a search-and-destroy mission. The dogs helpfully dug several hedgehogs out of the undergrowth where they were just settling in for a six-month snooze, but they found no sitting chook, grew bored and gave up. Eventually I did too. 'Good luck to you, chooky,' I said after a fruitless hour of bushwhacking, sat down, opened my haversack, withdrew the essentials and smoked them.

So when the missing chook finally came waddling up over the ridge on Saturday morning, it was with some relief that I noticed she was unaccompanied. Perhaps the rooster had found her ugly. But then out from beneath her peeped a beak, then a body like a fluffy ping-pong ball. It was followed by eight more, all black above and cream below. Ping went my heart, and then pong. I came over, in other words, all Pamela Anderson.

If I had any sense or consistency I would grab the whole brood while they're still catchable, sex them, find homes for the hens and wring the roosters' necks. But I'm no good at sexing chooks until it's obvious, and I'm even less good at neck-wringing. So I am in no position to criticise Pamela Anderson for her sentimental devotion to fur seal pups.

All I can legitimately say is that the sentimental appeal of baby animals is as strong an argument as I know for the truth of the theory of evolution, and that if you're going to be born onto this planet it's a cracking idea to resemble as closely as possible the offspring of the temporarily dominant species.

Reverend reasoning

Minutes of the AGM of the Intelligent Design Steering Committee, held somewhere on the intelligently designed planet earth.

Attendance: Those attending were the Reverend Peastem, the Very Reverend Drinklittle, the Astonishingly Reverend Archbishop Thimbledick and God.

Apologies: A handwritten apology for absence was received from G.W. Bosh (*sic*) and an apology in Latin from the late Pope (*sick*). Exactly the same apology was received from an unnamed source with the word Pope twinked out and replaced with the words 'Maxim Institute'. A telephone apology was received from The So-Reverend-It-Hurts Bishop Brian Tamaki who said he was there in spirit but was currently too busy ministering to his flock in the diocese of Tithe, Harley and Davidson.

Proceedings: The meeting opened with a prayer to which God listened intently and which he promised to answer just as soon as he'd answered the eight billion others that had landed simultaneously in his in-tray, most of which related to bird flu.

Minutes: The minutes of the previous meeting were read and approved. (*Mover, in a mysterious way: God. Seconder: God.*)

Point of order: The Reverend Peastem queried whether it was constitutionally permissible for the same person to move and second a motion, but God argued through the chair that he was in fact three persons. For evidence he quoted from the Bible, whereupon the chairman congratulated God on the reasoned nature of his argument. 'This is just the sort of deductive scientific method that we on the Intelligent Design Steering Committee seek to promote,' he said.

'Thank you,' said God, and asked for his gratitude to be recorded in the minutes.

'No, we thank you,' said the chairman and moved a motion that the committee thank God for intelligently designing everything. (*Seconder: Thimbledick.*) Peastem proposed that the motion be amended to thank God for intelligently designing 'everything except bird flu, oh, and perhaps leprosy, the Pakistan earthquake, Hurricane Wilma and genital warts' but the amendment did not find a seconder. The unamended motion was passed nem con. (*Abstention: God.*)

General Business: Only one agenda item had been tabled, the bid to have Intelligent Design included in the school science curriculum throughout the Western world. As chairman of the ad hoc subcommittee the Very Reverend Drinklittle reported that the campaign was proving successful because it had been intelligently designed. (*Laughter*) He attributed the momentum of the campaign to three specific causes, the first of which was branding. Changing the name from Creationism to Intelligent Design had completely altered its image in the public mind. It was now seen as a scientific theory rather than as a wishful belief. (*Coughing*) The second principal driver of success was funding. The extraordinary sums contributed by American business interests to support the campaign and also to establish propaganda bodies amusingly known as think-tanks had enabled the campaign to achieve unprecedented market penetration. 'In conclusion,' said the Very Reverend, 'it is the opinion of the ad hoc sub-committee that within ten years the average child will emerge from school unable to distinguish scientific method from a hamburger, and will consider both to be examples of Intelligent Design.' (*Applause, cheers, general acclamation, stamping of feet and an impromptu chorus of 'I'm no kin to the monkey, the monkey's no kin to me' enthusiastically conducted by Thimbledick with the femur of a chimpanzee.*)

The chairman congratulated Drinklittle on his sub-committee's success but reminded him that he had mentioned three contributing causes and wondered whether perhaps he might enlighten the assembly as to the nature of the third. In reply the Very Reverend merely looked towards God, bowed his head and said, 'Thank you.' (*Acclamation, blushes from God etc.*)

'Without your help,' said the Astonishingly Reverend, 'we would never have been able to stem the advancing tide of thought. Branding and money are all very well, but if we hadn't created you in our image, you would never have been able to create us in yours. (*Chorus of 'Great reasoning, Rev', 'Yeeha' and other expressions of religious awe.*) And if we hadn't intelligently designed you so that you could have intelligently designed us, we would never have felt justified in considering ourselves superior to the beasts of the field and the dogs of the kennel, nor would we have felt entitled to eternal life and all the rest of the fringe benefits that come from being your loved and intelligently designed children.

'Thanks to you, our current funding, and a multi-media advertising blitz scheduled for the spring, there is every reason to hope that the devil Darwin and his heretical dependence on observation and repeatable controlled experiments, will be beaten back to the superstitious jungle where it belongs and the Western world can advance on the sort of theocracy that the Middle East has had the good sense to maintain all along. And then we can have a real cracker of a war.'

There being no other business the meeting closed at 8.41pm with the traditional chorus: 'All things bright and beautiful' sang the happy steering committee,

All creatures great and small
All things wise and wonderful
The Lord God intelligently designed them all.

('Except,' added Peastem *sotto voce*, 'for bird flu, leprosy, the Pakistan earthquake, Hurricane Wilma and genital warts' but such was the general delight that nobody heard him.)

Nine to high noon

It's laughable. But I am not laughing. I am so down in the mouth that I am up in arms.

Here we are, six years into the twenty-first century, with the statute book so crammed with equal opportunity legislation that employers hardly dare breathe, and yet we have an organisation funded by taxpayers' money, an organisation that is effectively an arm of government, flouting both the spirit and the letter of the law so merrily and consistently that you would think its board of directors inhabited a different planet or the nineteenth century. Have all the struggles of the last fifty years been a pointless waste of energy and breath? It would seem so.

My beef, well, it should be obvious. Yet I have heard no one remark on it. Not a single commentator has dared to speak, to challenge the old girls' network. Perhaps the commentators think it is more than their life is worth. Well, my life is worth little and I am happy for it to become worth less. There are greater causes than personal worth. I shall speak. If bad things come of it, let them come. Let them rain down on my head. Let my skull be dented by insults. I don't have long to go now. Let my prone form be trodden to ribbons by stiletto heels from Andrea Biani. I shall be heard.

But then again, maybe I shall not. For I have been screaming about the sexism in our society for many a long year now, and a fat lot of good it has done. I have been a single plaintive voice deep in the forest and it seems that no one is listening except the secret police. What the secret police are doing in the forest is not immediately clear. Maybe they are just there to monitor me. If so, let them monitor. Let them record. Let them play those recordings in open court before a jury of my peers. I know no shame. I am dressed in the garb of righteousness and I stand with spine erect.

My beef? It is strong meat. It is hard to take on an empty stomach. I advise you to ingest a bowl of cereal, or a slice of toast with a little Marmite perhaps, before reading on. I mean to address the subject of National Radio.

You will have heard the story. Linda Clark, the presenter of *Nine to Noon*, the most influential programme on National Radio, has left her post to do I don't know what. It will not have escaped your attention that Linda Clark was and is a woman. In the chair at *Nine to Noon* she succeeded Kim Hill. Kim Hill was and is a woman. She in turn succeeded Maggie Barry. Maggie Barry was and is a woman. She in turn succeeded Sharon Crosbie. Sharon Crosbie was and is a woman.

And who has now been appointed to succeed Linda Clark? The appointee, whose name I have yet to commit to memory, was and is a woman. Is it just me, or is there a pattern here? Two women in a row could be considered a coincidence. Three, carelessness. Four, suspicious at best. Five, what? Will this line stretch out to the crack of doom?

I wish to be even-handed. I am happy to consider any argument for the defence. Could it be argued that *Nine to Noon* should be presented by a woman because the audience is primarily women? It could, but only by a dinosaur, a dinosaur that breathed its last deep in the forest alongside the secret police monitoring station somewhen around 1850. For since then the chain that bound women to the Shacklock has been snapped. Our society now pullulates with house-husbands, soft-voiced, jersey-wearing, right-thinking, left-voting, deeply considerate men. Marooned in the kitchen with only the squawks of toddlers to occupy them, these men are dependent on the radio for something to prevent their brains dissolving into blancmange. They deserve a break. They are the forgotten menials of our world, men whose unpaid labours are rewarded only by hearing that radio's top job has gone yet again to the oppressors. Why aren't they screaming?

They aren't screaming because they are daunted. Daunted by the women who scream, the women who easily find a voice on *Nine to Noon* to scream, as in a recent non-story, that women remain under-represented on the boards of private companies. A glass ceiling persists, scream the women. Even though the boards of directors exist only to serve their shareholders, even though it is in their interests to select the best person for the job, even though these boards have never received a smidgen of taxpayers' largesse, and even though very few women apply for positions on boards of directors and most of those few duly get appointed because the boards are terrified of the consequences of not appointing them, yet still the cry of injustice goes up. But when there is an unbroken line of female succession to a vital media throne, nothing. Just an eerie frightened silence, as in a forest, broken only by the crackle of the secret police listening post.

Okay, I'm coming out, my arms laid down, my hands up. Do your worst.

Little Miss Moss

Some dame rang, name of Moss. Said she'd never used a private dick before, but she was worried about her kid. Was there somewhere discreet we could meet?

'The Ankle,' I said. '7.30,' and hung up.

My clients like The Ankle. It's a low-down joint. No cameras, no questions, no risk of being spotted with a dick.

I got there early, wrapped myself round a tooth mug of rye and ordered snails for the dame. I never met the dame yet who ain't impressed by snails.

She was five corny minutes late. 'The name's Dick,' I said, taking her coat. It stank of money. I can live with that stink. 'But they call me Private. Tell me about this little angel of yours.'

'Oh, Private,' she said, 'it's my Kate. I'm so worried about her.'

'What's she do, your Kate?'

'She puts clothes on and takes them off.'

Wouldn't be the first dame to do that, I thought. 'Yeah,' I said out loud, 'but what's she do for a crust?'

'Just that,' said the Moss. 'She earns millions.'

I sucked air through my teeth and laced it with rye. 'Nice work if you can get it,' I said. 'So what's the beef?'

‘Oh, Private, haven’t you heard? She’s been accused of taking… boo hoo.’

I never heard of anyone taking boohoo before but I seen plenty dames cry. Only thing to do is look away till it blows over. Some of them like a good blub, same as some jerks like washing the car of a Sunday. While I waited I picked up a paper. It was three days old and wearing ketchup. The Ankle has seen better times.

This Kate Moss broad was all over the front page. But broad ain’t the word for her. She was six meals short of a decent curve. The modern look, I guess, but her story was as old as the Bible. Blonde makes good, gets sad and starts shoving chemistry up her hooter. I gave the tonsils another rinse.

Over the far side of the tablecloth things seemed to have quietened down. I offered the dame a slug of rye but she said she’d stick with the snails.

‘It’s the end,’ she sniffed. ‘Burberry’s gone. Chanel’ll be next, then Next, then…'

‘Slow down, Missus,’ I said, ‘you lost me at the first turn-off. Burberry? Are we talking fruit?’

‘We’re talking modelling millions and now it’s all gone just because of a little…’

‘Capisch,’ I said. ‘And now Kate’s hoovering up the Special K.’

‘If only,’ said the Moss. ‘But Kate’s never been one for breakfast.’

‘I ain’t talking breakfast, Mrs. This Special K’s a whole different stack of pancakes. Ketamine. That’s horse dope to you.’

‘Horse dope?’

‘Yeah, they jab it into Dobbin and he rolls over like an Italian tank. Can’t see the fun in it myself, but hey, it takes all sorts.’

‘But can you help me, Private? Can you steer my little girl off the drug-strewn road to ruin and back onto the highway to riches and the *Vogue* front page?’

‘Easy on the metaphors, lady,’ I said. ‘Leave the fancy stuff to me. In fact, leave everything to me, why don’t you.’

I didn't want to get her hopes up but an idea was sprouting in the back of my mind like a rubber plant. It was a crap simile but a cracking idea. It was the horse stuff that did it. My mind was going like the clappers and those clappers had rung a bell.

Half an hour later I'd shifted the Moss and was on the phone to New Zealand. I got some bint with a weird accent.

'Crowe, Fox and Bull,' she said.

'Hey listen, sister, if I'd wanted the farmyard I'd have rung Old McDonald. I want the guys behind this Oxy-shot business, you know what I mean.'

'Mr Crowe and Mr Fox are currently unavailable.'

'Okay, sister, just gimme the bull.'

'Very well, sir. At Oxy-shot we are proud to have employed NASA technology to create a liquefied hydrox compound supersaturated with stabilised diatomic oxygen molecules guaranteed to enhance well-being and boost vital oxygen supply. For a mere $200 a litre …'

'Yeah yeah, sister, so you're selling holy water.'

'Oh, Mr Dick, how did you see through us? Oh, this is terrible. Mr Crowe and Mr Fox will be furious. The whole business will …'

'Spare me the sob-along, sister,' I said. 'I ain't here to pour cold water on your cold water. Far as I'm concerned in this life, you do what you can get away with. What I wanna know is how you're gonna plug this Oxy-shot stuff. You with me? If not, listen up and listen up good.'

You know the rest. How Kate Moss became the face of Oxy-shot. Soon as I told her it was horse dope with no calories she went for it. Only too happy to guzzle the stuff in front of the camera. Sales went north like Apollo 16. Everyone wanted in on it. Oxy-shot for oxymorons. Kate got as skinny as a boy with breasts. My wallet went the other way. I even bought into the company. Crowe, Fox, Bull and Dick. It's got a kinda ring to it.

One

There are times when one's outrage boils like an unattended kettle, and now is such a time. There are times when one is obliged to speak up, and now is such a time. And there are times when one has no choice but to use the pronoun one.

'One' is such a magnificently pompous word. It levers itself up onto the stool of self-importance and sneers at the crowd. It brooks no possibility of being wrong. It implies that one represents all people who think right, and that the people who think wrong are insects to be swatted. Let them sneer, as insects are famous for doing, and let them biff their rotten fruit, ditto. When one is unquestionably right, one wears a decoration of rotten fruit as a war hero wears his medals.

The subject about which one wishes to express an opinion today is golf. One has expressed an opinion about golf before. Several years ago one suggested – no, one never suggests – one stated that recreational golf is as obvious an embodiment as one is ever likely to meet of human futility.

The reaction was predictable. One was accused, among other things, of despising golf because one wasn't any good at it. Naturally one dismissed such reaction with a haughty disregard and a noise best rendered on paper as harrumph, partly because that is the sort of thing one does, but mainly because one's accusers were golfers.

But today one is content to leave the recreational golfers to their folly, and instead one wishes to turn one's magisterial attention to professional golf. This, you will be astonished to hear, is golf played for money, and the first question one must ask is why anyone should pay someone else to play golf. Why, for example, do Volvo sponsor a golf tournament? Do they imagine that by associating themselves with professional golfers, they will sell more of their dreary Swedish cars to recreational golfers? The answer is yes. Furthermore they are bang right, which confirms everything one believes about golfers.

But the feature of the infantile wealth-laden circus of professional golf that has attracted one's magisterial attention is the US Masters – and oh, how that word sings with irony when one considers the people to whom the title is applied, but let that be.

The US Masters, as you may know, is played in Augusta, Georgia, a place of suffocating heat, cotton plantations and black people understandably singing the blues. Until remarkably recently the old boobies who run Augusta maintained the great Southern tradition of racial segregation, until indeed a freak by the name of Tiger Woods became so skilled at the great pointlessness that the boobies felt he was probably entitled to order a drink at their bar rather than just to pour it.

But this is not, as it happens, the point of one's moral outrage today, and neither indeed is Mr Woods, though his name does deserve a brief digression. Does the name Tiger appear on his birth certificate? Did the vicar lean over his crib and intone 'I christen this child Tiger. Long may he put'? One asks only because his name typifies the nonsensical and increasingly common myth-making of sporting nomenclature. In this region of the globe, for example, one notes the preposterously titled Canterbury Crusaders, and even more preposterously in the north of England there exists a rugby league team called the Leeds Rhinos. One can see the points of similarity between rugby league players and myopic pachyderms, but Leeds is hardly the high veldt. Still, let one leave that conundrum hanging in the air like summer cirrus, for one has a more substantial fish in the frying pan.

You will probably have seen Augusta on television, but if you are lucky enough not to have done, you can take it from one that it is faultless. It looks as Eden might have looked if Adam and Eve had had several thousand black servants and a set of Pings. The water features have the deep alluring blue of a Hollywood starlet's contact lenses. The turf is lusher than it has any right to be. The land has been so manicured, pedicured and facialed that it looks synthetic. In short, it's repellent.

The intention is clear. The setting is designed to imply that the beings who strut this course in their vile clothes are the denizens of arcadia. They are a higher order of being. One is supposed to admire them, and to wish to emulate them. At which thought one feels obliged to emit another harrumph.

But what has really got to one, what has caused one's long-simmering pot of distaste to become a furiously overboiling vat of loathing, was one's discovery that the authorities at Augusta are so serious about the fake image they wish to impart that, and one is not making this up, they dye the water. They dye the water on the golf course so that it looks nice and blue on television. In the face of which fact, to be quite frank, one is lost for words.

Hitch

Late on Friday night, I'm driving north up State Highway One, and somewhere beyond Temuka I see two figures by the road. They appear as silhouettes, young men slouching along the verge, somehow grotesque. They are hitching. I stop. I almost always do. As an ex-hitchhiker I feel obliged. Besides I am intrigued. Few people hitch late at night. I sniff a hint of adventure by proxy, of some sort of drama. Otherwise why should they be here in agricultural nowhere at eleven at night, far from pubs and lights? Also I am tired. I have felt my concentration drifting, my eyelids lowering. I could use some company.

I pull over on gravel 50 metres beyond them and shift a sweater and a burger wrapper from the passenger seat. The lads take a while to reach the car, then one taps hesitantly on the window. They are unsure whether I have stopped for them. A lift this late at night is too much to hope for. I lower the window.

'Where you heading for?'

'Ashburton.'

It's about 70 kilometres to Ashburton. I tell them to get in. They whoop with surprised delight.

One gets in the back, the other in the front. They're both about eighteen.

'Can we smoke?' asks the one in the back.

'Go ahead,' I say, and again they give a little whoop and chuckle. Both roll themselves a cigarette. 'Sweet,' says the one in the back.

'Sweet as,' says his mate.

'Your job,' I say, 'is to keep me awake. Tell me stuff. Tell me stories.'

'Stories?'

'Yeah, anything. Stuff that's happened to you. Just keep talking. You can start with why you're out here hitching.'

The lad in the front has a stainless steel curtain ring hooped through his lip. He tells me they'd driven that morning to Geraldine where they got drunk. They slept off the afternoon somewhere then discovered they'd lost the car keys. They walked the back roads to reach the main road.

'That's some walk,' I say.

The lad shrugs.

'What would have happened if I hadn't stopped for you?'

The lad shrugs again and laughs. 'Whatever,' he says, and I find myself admiring their insouciance. I suspect we all most admire the qualities we lack.

'Go on,' I say, 'tell me stories.'

And the lad in the front seat starts a rambling monologue that takes us all the way to Ashburton. The stories are all concerned with drink and with hating the police and above all with cars. He loves to drive. He lives to drive.

'Get a tank of gas and we just go. Four of us drove to Dunedin once, just for the hell of it. Did most of it at 150 clicks. Then we got a burger and went to Nelson. It was sweet.'

He tells me how the cops once followed him from Ashburton to Hinds when he was drunk and his car wasn't registered and he was temporarily without a licence. 'I was bricking it. I hate those bastards.'

In the back seat the other lad is silent. I glance back and he has fallen asleep, his head slumped on his shoulder and juddering against the window. His mate happily carries on, bathing in the stories of his own profligacy and recklessness. He's half boasting, half reminiscing. He tells me how he loves to pick up hitchhikers and terrify them by driving at enormous speed.

'Picked up these two chicks once near Orari and we went on the back roads and got up to 200 clicks and then did a whole load of donuts. They were screaming. Jeez, it was funny.'

I ask if all his friends drive like he does.

'Pretty much,' he says and tells me with wonder in his voice about his friend who's got a 300-horsepower car.

'Have any of your mates died?'

'No,' he says and seems surprised by the question.

His crowning story is semi-coherent. It involves being stopped three times in twelve hours by the police when he was driving an illegal vehicle. The police issued green stickers which, I gather, indicate that the car must not be driven, but he just peeled them off and drove on. He collected, he says, $4000 worth of fines in the one day. He is part proud, and part appalled that his freedom should be so circumscribed.

We reach Ashburton. I ask him where they want to be dropped off and he tells me one block back from the highway. I say I'll drive them to the door and again the lad gives a little whoop of almost childish glee.

'My missus will be up,' he says.

He wakes his mate. I pull up at their gate. They give me directions to get back to the highway and then thank me for the lift with surprising formality.

I watch them shamble up the drive, then I head for home. As I drive sedately through the night I reflect that though their behaviour is inexcusable, stupid, brutish and a lethal threat, I liked them. And a tiny part of me envied them.

Passion on the sofa

What were you doing at four o'clock on Monday morning? I was on a sofa doing love. And sweat. And dread. I was watching cricket.

England needed 130 runs to beat Australia. I could no more go to bed than I could vote for New Zealand First or eat broccoli.

Yes, yes, I know, cricket's only a game. I've heard the headmasters. I've met the sourpusses and the blue stockings and the pontificators in polo-neck sweaters. I've seen them tut and shake their clever heads and I've heard them mutter about bread and circuses. And I don't care. They're wrong. As wrong as spiritualists, as low-fat diets, as wrong as tourism.

This cricket mattered. It mattered viscerally. It mattered to the thousands who'd crammed into the tiny Trent Bridge ground to whoop and groan and lunch on their fingernails. And it mattered to me. As the bellbirds in the wattle announced the dawn's approach, and as the evil Warne went whittling through the English batting, his wrist curled like a cobra's neck, I was pinned to that sofa by the two most potent forces in the world. Nurture had me by the heart, nature by the crotch.

Nurture had me because I was dunked in cricket at the font. I have played a thousand games of cricket. I am intimate with its intricacies. Everything about it pleases me as only something can that you have known all your life. It has the reassurance of continuity. It is an old lover.

But nurture also had me because I'm English. Though I have lived abroad for almost all my adult life, and though I have taken out New Zealand citizenship, I have no choice. I am umbilically linked to England as Romanians are to Romania, Kiwis to these green and pleasant rocks and Eskimos to ice. It is not a question of liking or disliking one's place of birth. That place is mother. You have only one mother.

And I loved the England cricketers, if that is what is meant by fearing for their survival, praying for their triumph. It was easy to see national types in each of them: Marcus Trescothick as a cider-cheeked village policeman, heavy and rustic, slow on his feet but giving the ball a mighty simple thwack; Michael Vaughan as the colonel who doesn't know funk, who keeps himself in check with the imperturbable suavity of the ruling class; shag-haired Hoggard as a rural oik; and Flintoff as the giant and pasty-faced football hooligan who's crossed to the side of the angels and on whose behalf he now employs the clubbing thuggery he learned on the terraces.

All nonsense, of course. If any one of them were Australian he would seem typically Australian. Hoggard would be a Bondi-boy, Flintoff a crude colonial, Vaughan a remorseless chisel-chinned Ocker. But I don't and didn't care. My nurture made me love them for being English. And nature made me love the match.

That match unleashed a flood of feelings: the heart-grip of dread, the feeble candle-flame of hope, the rending passion of suspense, and great hooping yelps of joy, none of which I feel with such intensity in daily life. For what our peaceable and prosperous society has done is to bulldoze the alps of emotion. In making life safe it's flattened the peaks of delight and triumph, backfilled the chasms of terror.

We may imagine that safety's what we want, but we deceive ourselves. We crave trauma. We are hard-wired to crave it. Why else should people bungy jump or ski or run before the mad Pamplona bulls? We need the fork of lightning, the epic event, the momentary wrestle between death and glory. We have glands that exist solely to respond to fear and thrill and war. You can't argue with glands. There they squat, all fleshy and instinct-driven, ready to secrete adrenalin, testosterone and I don't know what other ungood chemicals that fire us up and make us feel.

And how well cricket caters to them. Cricket is life and death. The bowler is fate, the force of circumstance. He comes again and again, biffing missiles that threaten extinction, or juicy baited loops that tempt. And the batsman is us. The batsman must fail. In the end his stumps will fall. For every second of his innings he is one mistake from the grave, from the long trudge back to the necropolis of the pavilion, suddenly deprived of all the stuff that being alive brings with it. But before he fails, in the interlude before the stumps lie shattered, how brightly he can live. What scope he has for heroism, standing with his back to the abyss, defying fate by giving it a smack.

And England triumphed. My tribe won the war. When lumbering Farmer Giles gave fate and Warne a final cuff about the chops and hit the runs that won, I stood and spread my arms and filled my chest and bellowed like a beast. The dogs came running from the bedroom. They thought I was in pain or hunting. Poor simple creatures.

Thing and Thong

This film is the most certain winner since Phar Lap, but you wouldn't know it from meeting its director.

'I just enjoyed making it,' says Joe Bennett, draping himself over an armchair in the studio at the back of his modest Lyttelton property, 'and I hope people enjoy watching it. The critics can go hang.'

He smiles confidently, and he can afford to. If the crowds flock as expected, he stands to make millions from this low-budget remake of the 1930s classic *The Thing and the Thong*.

The plot will be familiar to all. The innocent heroine, dressed in a thong, travels to Quail Island on the trail of the mythical Thing only for it to prove a lot more than mythical. The Thong's companion gases the Thing into submission and tows it back to Lyttelton as a public exhibit, but the plan goes horribly wrong.

The key to the film's success lies in the casting. 'To play the Thing I needed something big, black and aggressive,' says Bennett, 'something to inspire dread, a haunter of nightmares, the beast in the back of the head that represents all our dark fears of the natural world, something that speaks of the untamed jungle, something to terrify us in the simplest, most atavistic way. Baz the Labrador seemed an obvious choice. He's very black and his teeth are very white. I did audition the cat, briefly, but it proved reluctant to take direction.'

And how did he make the Thing appear 10 metres tall? 'Nothing to it,' says Bennett. 'It's amazing what you can do with the zoom button on a Camcorder and a bit of cardboard scenery.'

The result is a beast that turns the Quail Island jungle into the Jungian subconscious. The Thing stalks the terrible uncharted landscape of the primitive human psyche.

And the battle with the giant spiny anteater? 'Pure chance,' says Bennett disarmingly. 'While we were shooting some cutaways, Baz wandered off and caught a hedgehog. He then tried to chew it. All I had to do was stick a model of Lyttelton behind him and we were away. I don't think Baz even noticed. He's a natural. The hedgehog, incidentally, was returned to the bush unharmed. The scene in which its head is ripped off and its innards splatter the lens was entirely generated by Dave down the road. He's a wizard with Photoshop.'

Was it the hedgehog that gave Bennett the idea for the scene in which the stegosaurus eats the Thong's companion? 'It was,' admits Bennett. 'Everyone knows there is no fossil evidence to suggest that the stegosaurus and the Labrador were coterminous, but hey, this isn't a documentary. We're talking mock-terrifying nonsense here, something to exploit the simplest and most irrational urges of the human species. There's no room for facts. Nor is there any room for words like coterminous. Keep it simple, that's always been my motto. Just fear, fighting and sex. It works.'

And how. As with the rest of Bennett's oeuvre, the violence is magnificent, almost loving, and the baddies are as obviously bad as smokers. But it's in the love interest that *The Thing and the Thong*, transcends all his previous work, including even the fabulously successful trilogy *Bored With All Things*.

In *Bored*, Bennett struggled to make the women convincing for the simple reason that there were none in the original text. But in this film the Thong matters every bit as much as the Thing.

'The Thong is the archetype of the girl next door,' says Bennett, 'so I cast the girl next door. She was cheap and keen and she has a thing for Baz which I think comes across in the movie.'

It does, so much so that I challenge any viewer not to weep at the climactic scene. The Thing has climbed to the roof of Lyttelton's iconic Timeball Station with the Thong in his paw. And just when the worst possible ending seems inevitable, the Thing looks down at the terrified Thong and is smitten. The Thing goes soft. It falls in love.

'It transmogrifies on the instant,' explains Bennett, 'from giant black ogre to paradoxically alluring bad-boy lover. The Thing becomes the chest-thumping alpha male, the protective hairy father figure that every woman craves. Forget your metrosexuals, your sensitive new agers, your house-husbands and empathisers. Here is manhood in the raw. Every female heart will melt. Women aren't as complex as they like to make out.'

When I suggest that some critics might find the film a little dumb, Bennett just laughs. 'Course it's dumb. It's a dumb industry. If I'd made it all cerebral, using words like transmogrifies or paradoxical, what do you think would have happened? Precisely. No queues at the theatres and, more importantly, no merchandising.'

He throws open a cupboard in his studio and out tumbles a cascade of cuddly Things, vibrating Things, blow-up Thongs, blood-drenched video games, 'I slept with the Thing and the Thong' bumper stickers and movie-tie-in special-edition chocolate bars.

'Arouse Dad, scare the kids, and make Mum weep and you can sell the cretins anything,' says Bennett. 'You don't shift stuff like this by aiming high.'

Welcome

Dawn. I greet the new day with a cough by Benson and Hedges. I fill and fire the coffee machine, then pad downstairs, a dog at my feet. I am going to fetch the paper. In my fancy new house I pause at the door that grants what is known in real estate circles as internal access to the garage. When I use the term 'real estate circles' I am quoting Dante.

On the far side of the door I hear faint squeaking. I prick my ears. The dog hears it too but doesn't prick his ears because labrador ears don't prick. They just arch slightly at the leading edge, like eyebrows, lending the dog a winsome appearance. I pay no attention to the winsomeness of the dog. I pause, pricked. The dog pauses, floppily intent.

The squeaking is odd, faint, repeated, very high pitched, as if the garage were full of pre-pubescent burglars. I look at the dog. Despite being a labrador he is territorial. He is keen to go. I open the door. Having spent twenty years teaching, there is a part of me that would like to see a territorial labrador among trapped pre-pubescents.

I see no pre-pubescents. I see a black flicker, then another. The dog sees them too. Side by side we stand and look. I have a garageful of swallows.

It takes a while to decide exactly how many there are. They dart and glide and dive and swoop, now here, now gone, now under, now over, flipping, arcing, rolling, turning, touching nothing, skirting everything, always squeaking, like bats. They wheel round the lumbering bulk of my car, impossibly precise. It's a big garage. They fill it. There are two of them.

I've seen them before. Last week they came to the garage one evening and they returned again and again to the corner by a high shelf of books that I have stored there because I cannot burn or sell them. Sometimes the swallows would perch on the books, like tiny feathered spearheads, suddenly immobile, faultless. They didn't perch for long. Swallows never seem to perch for long.

Ted Hughes was good on the swallow. He called it 'a whiplash swimmer, a fish of the air'. The swallow was 'the seamstress of summer. She scissors the blue into shapes and she sews it', and the line has the same swing as the flight of the bird.

But swallows aren't seamstresses. They are murderers. That scissoring is feeding. They are catching insects. Only seriously saintly people have sympathy for insects. I don't. Swallows don't. Insects are countless, unpretty, insensate. Swallows are feathered and pretty and closer to us.

I see swallows often when fishing. They whirl and dive and squeak an inch above the water, spearing invisible insects, being swallows. Being swallows is all they do. Simplicity in feathers.

I expect the dog to bark and make a clumsy hopeless charge at the birds. But like me he just stands, following their flight with the great hulk of his head. The swallows seem like a privilege, a blessing, a kindness, a gift, sleek and untroubled. You never see an old swallow. Any failure, any decay, any slip from perfection, any loss of aerobatic deftness, and the swallow can't feed and the swallow dies. But I've never seen a dead one. Swallows inhabit only summers.

My new house is seriously fancy. I press a button and the garage door groans, rumbles and opens. When it is a quarter open, the swallows whip down and through the gap like the flung swings of a fairground ride. They are gone.

Down the zigzag drive I pad with the dog, the half-light sweet with bellbirds. The trees are wet. The air is held promise that the day will dissolve. The paper lies furled on the drive. The dog fetches it in his great soft mouth, his teeth as precise as a swallow's flight. He brings it up to me, his body swinging, writhing with the pleasure of capture. I take the paper. He lets it go gently. Not even a dent in the cellophane from those great white teeth. Many a time I've seen those teeth break a possum's neck. Instantly.

The garage is empty. Up to the kitchen. The coffee machine stands charged and steaming. I pour and sit and unwrap the paper. Newsreader salaries, newsreader squeaking, Hayley Westenra's crush, house prices, spitting, terror of bird flu, Winston Peters. I lay the paper aside, sip the good coffee, light a cigarette, and shut my eyes to see the swallows. I hope they come back. I hope they nest with me.

Eggdog

Last week I wrote that I couldn't find the eggs that my chooks had been laying. I announced that I was going to train my dog to sniff them out. The dog is a labrador.

A friend who knows the dog well rang to ask if I was also planning to teach Winston Peters coherence.

'One thing at a time,' I said.

The first thing was to manipulate the dog's mind. I had to associate eggs with good consequences. For a labrador, good consequences are defined as food. Food is defined as anything carbon-based. That definition includes pizza boxes, vomit and the connective tissue on possums that died last month.

Not having any pizza boxes or dead possums on me, and being unable these days to vomit on demand, I armed myself for the great egg hunt with a pocketful of boiled liver. You and I may not consider boiled liver to be food but we are not labradors.

I stood before the dog and held out an egg for him to sniff. The dog immediately sniffed the pocketful of liver. He wagged his tail. When I say tail I mean body. If a labrador is happy its tail starts at its waist. If a labrador smells liver its tail starts at its ears. The only reason it doesn't wag its nose is that the nose is locked onto the liver.

'No,' I said and I offered the egg again. At the same time I said 'egg'.

I don't know why I said 'egg'. 'Egg' is not a command with which the dog is familiar. The dog did what he always does when he is unfamiliar with a command and there is liver about. He sat.

'Good boy,' I said because at least he was trying. I gave him a piece of liver. From a labrador's point of view this was excellent. From a training point of view it was not.

I offered the egg again. The dog continued to sit because sitting had proved an effective tactic. I waved the egg about a bit and made encouraging noises. The dog stood up to sniff the egg. I was delighted. Involuntarily I said 'egg' again. The dog sat.

I swore. The dog wagged his tail. When a sitting dog wags its tail it is like a horizontal windscreen wiper.

I made a mental note to stop saying 'egg', then offered the egg once more. When the dog sniffed it, I gave him liver. We did this six times. We were getting somewhere. I told the dog to stay and I placed the egg behind the sofa three yards away. I returned to the dog and performed my 'seek' gesture, which involves turning my palms upwards and shrugging my shoulders in the manner of an Inspector Clouseau who has run low on clues. (I also pull a puzzled face although I am not sure that this is important to the dog.) The dog went straight behind the sofa.

It did not take long to get the yolk out of the carpet because the dog had lapped up most of it. I disposed of the bits of shell, and fetched another egg. I considered hard-boiling it, then had a clever idea. I fetched a roll of sellotape.

The dog watched with fascination as I wrapped the sellotape tightly round the egg, then leapt with enthusiasm to catch the slither of egg white. He got the yolk whole.

I took more care sellotaping the next egg, then made the dog stay and hid the egg behind the curtain. I told the dog to seek and he went straight behind the curtain.

It is mildly amusing watching a dog trying to get sellotape out of its teeth. In the end I had to give him a hand.

Thereafter I took a tip from airport sniffer dogs, and kept the dog on a lead. I would hide an egg, return to the dog, do a quick Clouseau, then snatch up the lead and follow. When the dog found the egg I pulled him up short and fed him liver. He thought this an excellent if mysterious game.

We graduated to outside. I hid eggs under pansies, in the shed, behind a rusting spade. The leashed dog found them all and ate only one of them and that was my fault because I got carried away with my Peter Sellers routine.

I ventured deeper into the garden in search of tougher hiding places. By the fence is a stand of bamboo. I swept aside the lower branches, stooped to place an egg on the ground and then stopped. In front of me was a clutch of two dozen eggs, laid in neat concentric circles. I yelped with delight and the dog came running.

'Look, Baz,' I said, 'eggs!'

Baz sat.

Right, Winston, come here and listen up.

Apocalypse Now

With World War III enticingly round the corner, or at least simmering in the nearby parish of possibility, thanks to a few Danes who got fed up with being ignored on account of their being Danes, it's a fine time for apocalyptic visions. And when it comes to visions, apocalyptic is my speciality. I like them juicy, involving imploding nation states, a sky full of fireballs, televisual celebrities fleeing down lanes in their underpants pursued by wolverines, evangelists with herpes, missionaries in the pot, the pot on the fire, and the fire being the city of Paris or anywhere else that's got a Disneyland. And that's just for hors d'oeuvres. These warm February evenings I sit on the browned hills of Lyttelton and conjure delicious apocalyptic images to bask in, images such as advertising executives being forced to beg by the side of the road dressed only in discarded cereal packets and ceaselessly mouthing their own promotional jingles in the hope of wringing a farthing of sympathy from the passing Lord of All Things Apocalyptic, who, as it happens, is me.

I have a vision, too, of heaping spectacular indignities on any linguistic pedant I can snare, the sort of person who would dare to suggest that the 'me' at the end of the last paragraph should be 'I'. He or she, and on balance I plump for both – he with a cardigan and too many insurance policies, she with no make-up and a feigned enthusiasm for Bach – will be winched above a crowd of yellow-toothed peasants and then required to repeat in tones of reverence suitable for addressing the Lord of All Things Apocalyptic, 'In the English language, the copula nominative is a dead duck.' Then, just to further the cause of their humiliation, they will have to split five infinitives in under five seconds, and chant 'prepositions are for ending sentences with' to the tune of 'I've Got a Lovely Bunch of Coconuts', before being lowered to the jeering mob who will do as they wish with them, the Lord of All Things Apocalyptic having turned his majestic attention to, let's see now, media matters.

During my apocalypse all perpetually cheerful radio disc jockeys, with or without phoney American accents, will be impaled on synchronised turntables and required to grin while listening to the latest Justin Timberlake on infinite replay. They will simultaneously be obliged, by force if necessary and I hope it is, to use a nicely ironic old-fashioned record-player stylus to tattoo on their foreheads in pink capitals, 'Any song containing the word "baby" is an offence against public decency', and they will not be allowed a dictionary to help with the spelling. Because my apocalypse will not only be awash with righteous indignation, it will also be jolly good fun.

Anyone associated in any way, however peripheral, with any television programme involving renovating a garden, a house, a fat woman's body or a feral child will get to learn the full extent of my wrath, and I refuse to ruin the surprise by telling them what that is except that it involves a weasel, several long-handled garden implements and a can of clarified butter that, with delicious cruelty, proves to be empty. And any 'lifestyle-show presenter' celebrating the joys of local and/or seasonal and/or organic produce by taking a forkful, chewing, looking at the camera as if transported to a world of unlimited sexual gratification, and saying, 'mmmm, it's to die for', will discover that in my apocalypse this cute little metaphor is taken literally.

I shall also be paying close apocalyptic attention to sport. Anyone under the age of retirement found playing bowls will be obliged to retire immediately and condemned to spend the remainder of their days in the overheated television room of The Eventide Home for People Who Have Considered Voting for Winston Peters, where they will be joined as soon as I can find her by the woman who designed the new body-hugging All Blacks shirt that makes rugby players look like technicians on the USS *Enterprise*. But anyone expressing interest in surfing as a spectator sport or attending any form of motor-racing will be spared retribution on the grounds that they have already achieved a level of moral and emotional degradation that even the Lord of All Things Apocalyptic is frankly unable to enhance.

I could go on, of course, and I shall. The travel business, for example, will be required to advertise holiday destinations with pictures taken in the rain. And posters of winsome smiling locals in indigenous costume will come with a compulsory warning underneath saying 'These people are poor. They are smiling at your wallet.' Ads for airlines will show overweight people in Hawaiian shirts queuing for hours to be x-rayed and body-patted in some synthetic airport before being crammed into a plane where their nearest fellow adventurer will be a baby with colic and lungs like an air-raid siren.

But 800 words are insufficient to give more than a taste of my apocalyptic menu. Keep up the good work, you Danes. Together we'll get this show on the road. You know it makes sense.

Flies say no

Seven in the morning and the sun is rumbling over the ridge to toast the creamy flanks of my house and the black flanks of my dogs. It will herd the dogs into the shade and it will haul forth their pink, wet tongues to pulse through the heat of day. And it will quicken the flies. I am at peace with the house and the dogs, but I am at war with the flies. I hate them. I kill them without compunction. I gloat over their corpses. My hatred is pure and good.

The dogs get bones each morning and the flies get the bones for the rest of the day. The flies gather while the dogs are chewing. They circle the dogs, corruption on wings. The noise that the flies carry tingles the hairs in my ears.

The dogs are on my side, on the side of creation. They snap at the flies, teeth clashing with a precise and potent threat. The flies evade the great teeth with mocking ease. They fizz a few inches away, hungry, impatient, eager to corrupt, certain of victory. They will inherit the bones and the earth. They want both now. They are entropy. Black and hairy, shrunken nightmares fashioned into flesh. And what flesh. No meat to them. No honest red muscle. No haunch. Swat a fly and there's only an ooze of stuff, like pus. Pus that draws another fly to perch on its brother with brittle suckered feet, and to feast.

Flies zigzag everywhere. Into corners, seeking residue, remains, decay, the gone and the was. Into my kitchen, revelling in my slovenliness, the crumbs around my toaster, the buttered knife in the sink, the dregs and spills, the offal of living. They worry too at the seal on the fridge, wanting the good, wanting to make it bad. I keep fly swats everywhere, like a paranoid billionaire whose mansion bristles with guns. I am always ready to defend by attacking. I swing wildly, carving the air, enraging the flies. The buzz shifts up through the gears, through the octaves. The rage is good. It drives them full tilt into glass. On glass I can kill. And I do. Three, four, five flailings of the swat, then the tiny grim crunch and sudden silence. The sweetness of death.

I, who am not squeamish, hate to handle the stilled and weightless corpse. I shovel it up with the quivering swat-tip, unload it into the sink, turn on the tap. Gone. But never gone, never while summer lasts. Summer is flies. The unstoppable horde, the flip-side of summer growth, the antonym of good, of love, of yes. Flies say no.

And then, last week, a woman told me of a fly-trap. 'It kills,' she said, 'and it kills good. We get no flies.' I wanted no flies. I sourced the fly trap, drove 15 miles to buy it, brought it home like booty. I assembled it according to the instructions with eager impatient fingers. The flies fizzed around me as I worked, checking out their fate.

A 10-litre paint pail, a hole cut into the lid. Into the paint pail a few inches of water and a heart, a sheep's heart, bought from the butcher for pennies. The heart has to be weighted down beneath the water, to be slowly cooked by the heat of the day, to make soup. For the weight I used the head of a hammer. Then over the hole goes the fly trap, a frisbee of plastic with a vane of sorts on its topside and a well in its centre and holes to release the smell of soup. The same holes let the flies in but not out. Lured by a rotting heart. So apt. So very good.

The trap takes one warm day to mature. That day was yesterday. It caught no flies. But five minutes ago I left the keyboard and my cool basement study and I climbed the stairs into the day's warmth and, with dogs watching incuriously from the shade, I studied my trap. Whoever invented it had read my mind. He made the frisbee transparent so I could see the doomed flies, circling in the pail, drenched, saturated in the smell they love, and quite unable to escape from it, done in by their own desires. Lovely. There were three of them. When darkness comes the pail will cool, the vapour will condense and the flies will tumble from the sheer walls and they will drown, unseen and unlamented.

In time the decomposing flies will supplant the heart as bait. The flies will flock to their own necropolis. I cannot wait.

I went to the kitchen to make a celebratory coffee. A fly fizzed past my scalp, perched on the frying pan. I reached for the swat. The war is never won. But in this house at least there is growth in the armoury of good. We angels fight. We must.

White brain, black body

John joined the dogs and me on a late-night walk. A gibbous moon cast shadows like scissored black paper.

'Nice gibbous moon,' I said, on the principle that there's no point in knowing words if you don't flaunt them.

'Gibbous?' said John, which was the correct response.

Feeling the delicious glow of condescension, I began a definition of gibbous but John wasn't listening.

'See that star there,' he said, pointing, 'the reddish one?'

'Yes,' I lied.

'It's called Daktari.'

'Daktari,' I said, scattering exclamation marks like an asteroid shower. 'They've named a star after Dakbloodytari.'

Readers under the age of thirty-five may stop reading now. Go on, off you go to the pop-music reviews, both of you. It's time for middle-aged nostalgia.

Way back in the 1960s when the world was still in primary school, *Daktari* was a television programme set in Africa. It featured white men who wore safari suits and black men who didn't. The black men didn't because they were children of nature and the sun was a blessing on their lean taut flesh. Hard to imagine it now, of course, but back in those days of innocence and the Vietnam War, people thought the sun was a good thing.

Daktari was a vet and the principal white man. The safari suit spared the viewer the sight of Daktari's sloppy belly, but it also emphasised the important bit of Daktari, which was the bit sticking out the top of the safari suit. Daktari might not have had a lean taut body but he did have a white man's head. What he did with that head made him the bwana.

Black men used their heads differently. They used their mouths for grinning and they used their eyes for steering through the bush as they ran from wherever it was that they'd discovered a crisis to wherever it was that Daktari lay swinging in his hammock. When they got there they used their mouths to shout.

'Daktari, Daktari,' they shouted, 'come quickly. There is a crisis over here so please put down the gin, climb off the hammock and into your safari suit and don't forget to bring that throbbing brain of yours to solve the problem, because, sadly, we're only Africans, massa, and though our bodies may be lean and taut, and our teeth perhaps a shade whiter than yours, when it comes down to it we're just tribal meatheads.'

'On my way,' said Daktari, leaping into his Land Rover without spilling his gin. The Land Rover was a motorised safari suit. It was also the only way Daktari could keep up with Africans.

If Daktari got lost in the Land Rover he just called on a black man to sniff the ground or spot a broken twig or to take a compass bearing with the entrails of a snake and then he was off once more towards the problem that he would solve with his enormous white brain.

The only help Daktari got came not from his decorative female assistants, nor yet from the grinning black boys, but from animals. His two top animals were Clarence the cross-eyed lion and Judy the gibbering chimp.

There was a well-worn bit of footage that showed Judy gibbering and jumping up and down in a state of agitation. This footage was spliced into the programme whenever there was danger in the camp. The danger was always poachers. And clever Judy always spotted them first.

I have since heard that Judy had to have her teeth removed because she kept biting the cast. Perhaps it was at the dentist's that they shot the footage of her in a state of agitation. If so, neither fact was well publicised at the time. Everybody loved Judy.

Everyone loved Clarence even more. Clarence had his own cross-eyed point-of-view camera. It showed everything in blurry stereo. Clarence frightened poachers, but actually he wouldn't hurt a fly, perhaps because he could see two of them.

The animals were devoted to Daktari, or, in Clarence's case, to the Daktari twins. Daktari in turn was devoted to Clarence and Judy. But he was also devoted to all the wild animals in Africa who constantly needed his help to get by.

How the animals of Africa had got by for a trillion years before Daktari rolled up in his safari suit was a mystery. Presumably Clarence's forebears kept picking the wrong prey out of two and starved to death horribly, while Judy retained her teeth but got poached, then boiled or fried.

Daktari was a programme for children. And I loved it. At eight years old I never missed an episode. What I didn't notice at the time was that *Daktari* was sentimental, patronising, white supremacist propaganda. It portrayed Africa as a giant game park populated by nice animals and child-like humans, a place that needed to be saved from itself. Is it a coincidence that this also happens to be the view of Africa that has been adopted by the adult Western world throughout my lifetime with disastrous consequences? I'm not sure that it is. The stories we tell to children are potent things.

'I'm astonished,' I said to John, 'they named a star after *Daktari*. It was sentimental, patronising, white…'

'Not Daktari,' said John, 'Antares.'

'Oh,' I said. And we walked on in silence beneath the gibbous moon.

The threshold of the ginge

I wish to propose a toast. On a Tuesday morning in snow-bound Lyttelton I am raising a glass with bubbles in it to the boffins of Louisville University, Kentucky. They are my US Cavalry. They may have arrived forty years too late to do my psyche much good, but I am still grateful. They have confirmed something that I have always known but that no one else has ever believed. I'm sensitive. I feel pain more than you feel pain. Now the boffins have revealed why. I'm sensitive because I'm a redhead.

I'm not a redhead any more. I'm a baldhead with wisps. But those wisps are the remnants of a head of hair that forty years ago was visible from space. It was the bane of my childhood. Goldilocks, they called me, or Ginge or Carrot-top. As a child, if I wanted to hide from my mother at the supermarket I just burrowed into a display of oranges.

And I did want to hide from my mother because my mother wanted to take me to the dentist. As far as I recall, most of my childhood consisted of being dragged to the dentist, heels dug in like a recalcitrant puppy, wailing like a world-ranked professional mourner, and smelling faintly of oranges. I wailed and dug because the dentist hurt.

Our family dentist was called Mr Wisher. I wasn't alone in dreading Mr Wisher. He was Victorian and brutal. His drill was operated by a bicycle chain that he wound with his spare hand. The waiting room door had a bolt on it.

But then we shifted to a twentieth-century dentist called Nice Mr Mabberly. Nice Mr Mabberly gave anaesthetics and even asked what flavour you wanted. I always asked for strawberry and didn't mind the injection. But then he drilled and I did mind the drill. I minded because it hurt. 'Tut tut,' said my mother and Nice Mr Mabberly as they peeled me from the ceiling. 'It can't hurt. You've had an injection.' They were wrong. It did hurt. And now forty years on I know why.

'Redheads,' says Louisville University, Kentucky, and I'm quoting, 'need more local anaesthetic at the dentist than the general population.' And that's science. So suck on that, Nice Mr Mabberly. Suck on that, Mother (though I mean that in the kindest possible way).

The reason it hurt, according to the lovely boffins, is that carrot-tops have a special gene. It is Celtic in origin and it dictates that we have 'a lower pain threshold'. Bang right, boffins, and thank you. My pain threshold is subterranean.

At university I took up boxing. I did it mainly to prove to myself that I wasn't the wuss that everyone had told me I was because of my threshold. I impressed the trainer with my walloping of the punch bag and was the first of the novices to be given a bout. I can still remember my opponent. He was an aristo called Rupert. He had mouse-coloured hair. The bell rang and I hit Rupert. I hit him hard and repeatedly. Boxing was lovely and I was good at it. I was mentally lifting the world light-heavyweight crown, the cheque that came with it, and the label of 'wuss' from my shoulders, when Rupert hit me. He hit me on the side of the head and then on the nose and then on the side of the head again. 'Ow,' I said and then 'ow' and then 'ow'. Of course I should have hit Rupert back and I briefly considered doing so but it's difficult to hit someone when you've turned your back on him and covered your head with your hands. It's also hard to take aim when you're crying. I jumped out of the ring, went home and never came back. That night my pillow whispered 'wuss'.

It was the same with rugby. I liked rugby but I couldn't bear to be rucked. 'A little tickle-up with the studs', they called it. I called it excruciating. I would let people know it hurt. 'Wuss,' they said. 'Worse than wuss,' they thought. If only they'd known. If only I'd known.

In cross-country I used to get a stitch. A schoolmate who was good at running told me that the way to deal with a stitch was to keep running until it went away. Ha. Same as if you're stabbed on the way to work the best thing to do is to carry on as normal. When I got a stitch I had no choice but to lie down in the mud like a dying lamb and bleat at the Great Ewe in the sky. 'Oi, Ewe,' I'd bleat, 'why me?'

How easy it would have been for the Great Ewe to tell me about my gene. But no. It took science to do that, as usual. Here's mud in your eye, Kentucky, and thank you.

Follow that child

Are you afflicted by visions? No, nor am I, but the moment I read about the website where parents could track the performance of their children at school, my head filled with an image I couldn't repress.

The scene is a suburban living room where a fifteen-year-old boy called Desideratum is leaning over the back of an Italian leather lounge suite from Harvey Norman. He is watching an episode of NZ Idol *with transparent boredom, while his father swats at his backside with a rolled-up copy of* Empathetic Parenting.

Desideratum: Dad, this is hurting you a lot more than it hurts me.

Dad: (*pausing for breath*) Son, if you're suggesting that I, your very own biological father by in vitro fertilisation, have been enfeebled by the redistribution of gender roles in the early twenty-first century, then all I can say is, wait till your mother gets home.

Desideratum: (*idly flicking the remote control to the 34-inch plasma television until pausing on a channel dedicated to women's golf. A woman in immaculately pressed shorts and a pink eye-shade is assessing a put before a gallery of ten fat Californians.*) No, Dad, I was just saying that it doesn't hurt.

Dad: When your mother sees your NCEA progress reports on that website the school has set up in order for nice middle-class parents like us to obsessively monitor the development of our precious only child to whose welfare we have sacrificed fifteen years of our lives, and in particular when she sees your performance in Achievement Standard 2.8 in the subject of English, well, I wouldn't want to be in your training shoes, however hi-tec they may be. Meanwhile perhaps I can get a bit more force into this thrashing by wearing the tails of my shirt outside my trousers in the manner of weather presenters and other icons of contemporary masculinity.

Desideratum: Fair enough, Dad. But while we're waiting for Mum, do you want to watch the golf, or one of the seventeen available programmes on renovating a house or ...?

But his question is drowned by the growl of a 4-litre sports utility vehicle drawing up in the internal-access garage, and the approaching clack of 4-inch heels.

Mum: Darlings, I'm home. What a relief it is every day to discover that you have survived the last eight hours in this hostile world where we live amid all the fruits of consumer luxury and yet somehow feel more scared and rudderless than our remote forefathers did in the jungle and ...oh, what's going on here?

Dad: It's Desideratum. I've been tracking...

Desideratum: And that's another thing. Why did you have to give me such a ridiculous name?

Mum: Don't interrupt your father, Desideratum. As for your name, I've told you before that it's the fashion these days to give children unique names. It emphasises that you are the ultimate accessory, available to no other magazine-reading couples in the whole of the Western world. But meanwhile, what's all this about?

Dad: In Achievement Standard 2.8 in the subject of English, Desideratum only achieved the standard rather than achieving it with excellence. In other words, he structured and organised information in an appropriate written format, but he failed to structure and organise it in an appropriate and effective written format.

Desideratum: (*to Dad*) Snitch.

Mum: I see. So what have you got to say for yourself, you wicked child?

Desideratum: Nothing.

Mum: Nothing? Nothing! Is that all we get for sacrificing fifteen...

Desideratum: Dad's been through all that.

Mum: Silence! Do you ever consider what we've gone through for you? We ignored the risk of childish damage to our Italian leather lounge suite from Harvey Norman. We smothered you with affection, catered to your every whim, half drowned you in toys, chauffeured you from macramé class to trumpet lesson to jujitsu competition so that you never had to walk anywhere, and provided you from the age of five with a full-time emotional counsellor and life coach with unrestricted access to Ritalin, Prozac and other faddish drugs. How many other children have had your advantages?

Desideratum: Most of them in my school.

Mum: (*ignoring him*) And yet this is how you thank us, is it? You callously fail to pay attention to the word 'effective' in the rubric for an NCEA achievement standard.

Desideratum: But, Mum, the word 'effective' doesn't mean anything. It's claptrap, Mum. It gives the illusion of objectivity, but in reality it remains subjective. NCEA progress reports are not reports of progress. They're sops to the vogue for assessment, the obsessive need to measure. They represent, ultimately, a distrust of both teacher and taught. And as for the website, Mum, it represents the same fundamental fear and distrust. Kids need space, Mum. In the end they have to escape the parental yoke.

Mum: (*roaring*) Enough. Go to your room at once. (*Dad obediently trots off. Mother and son are left facing each other over the Italian leather lounge suite from Harvey Norman. Mum unbuckles her Italian leather belt from Zambesi. It's a chunky thing.*) Desideratum, my darling, this is going to hurt us both.

Rod and gut

I told her I had been away fishing with friends. She snorted.

'That's so…' she said, then paused and I saw the muscles at the top of her cheeks tense and bulge as she sought the best word to express her distaste. She found the word. 'It's so primitive,' she said. 'Fishing is just primitive.'

'Mmm,' I said and sipped at my fancy foreign lager. She was drinking the same fancy foreign lager, but had put it aside on the bar so she could reinforce words with gestures. The gestures were not loving gestures, not peaceable gestures.

'There you are, a bunch of sad blokes finding yourselves washed up on the infertile beach of middle age and feeling castrated by a changed world, by the rise of women, by us having seen through you and being no longer obliged to suck up to you and warm your slippers and tolerate your smugness, so off you toddle into the bush in pursuit of fish that you don't need, solely so that you can beat your chests and play King Kong in the theatre of your own mind. It's primitive, regressive, wrong.'

She paused. She wanted a reaction. She wanted me to toss another log on the fire of her disdain.

'Mmm,' I said.

'Is that it?' she said.

'It's the word primitive that puzzles me,' I said. 'If, by primitive, you mean wading into the wide flat of a river early on an autumn evening and standing thigh-deep in the water waiting for the light to fade amid bush, bush that's grown and died and fallen and rotted without purpose for thousands of years, for hundreds of thousands of years, and as the sun's last rays quit the tips of the trees and the night seeps in and a weka screams and a morepork calls from deep in the bush and is answered from somewhere deeper, the mirrored surface of the river flat starts to dimple with the hatching of the caddis flies and those flies infest the air and cling to the brim of your hat and alight on your lips and cheeks and wriggle down the neck of your shirt and the back of your shirt so that you writhe and swat, and what may be an eel knocks against your leg, but then you hear the first splash of a trout rising to those hatching flies and all thoughts of discomfort melt on the instant and you become taut, intent, aware only of fish and water, and the rises become more frequent and are visible in the dark as concentric glinting swirls of steely water and you peel the line from your reel and cast with all the delicacy you can muster and your fly lands invisibly on the black water and in the area where it ought to be you hear a splash and you strike and either the water erupts into hooked fish or it doesn't, if that's what you mean by primitive, then yes, fishing is primitive.'

I took a sip of lager. So did she. Her eyebrows told me to go on, to dig my grave a little deeper. I picked up the spade.

'Or if, by primitive, you mean arriving one morning at the flood plain of a big river, and you stand on the stop bank to scan the water for the dark torpedoes of trout and to assess where it will be possible to cross and where it will be best to fish and what direction the wind is coming from, and the morning is bright with the promise of fishjoy, and you slither down the bank and step into the cold fringe of the river's vastness and feel the sheer weight of the water against your legs, the huge unstoppable tonnage of water pouring off the mountains, hundreds of thousands of tons of it on the constant move, and you are there to raid it, to try to pluck fish from its hugeness, and all that you have to raid it with are your wits, a 10-foot rod, a line that tapers to a nylon point too fine to see, and at its tip a barbed nymph the size of a maggot, so that your venture seems not so much an act of hunting as an act of bravado against monstrous odds, an impertinence, an audacity, and yet against these odds you cast your puny line into a likely flow and the line tip veers to one side and you strike and feel the thrilling chunk of a fish that plunges faster than thought towards deeper water, and your reel screams and your rod bends and you whoop whoop whoop for the fierce joy that has hold of you, if that is what you mean by primitive then you and I look on that word in different ways. You think it bad. I don't.'

And we both sipped at our lager.

Speak to us

Speaking puzzles me.

In private I speak a lot because my dogs find my voice mellifluous, my opinions incisive and my wit uproarious. But I am also sometimes asked to speak in public.

Some people offer me money to speak. Others offer me the pleasure of their company, a cup of tea and an aptly named rock cake.

The occasions that I am asked to speak at often surprise me. One was a fund-raising event at a suburban tennis club. It sounded polite. It turned into an all-in brawl. At the end of the evening furniture was being broken over skulls. On the phone the following morning the tone of the club secretary seemed to imply that I was partly responsible.

On another occasion a rugby league club invited me to address its members. I expected a male audience of a down-to-earth nature. What I did not expect was to be the warm-up act for a strip show. I still believe I should have been informed. Two minutes into my speech the audience became impatient to move on to the next item of the agenda. They expressed that impatience with words and then missiles. I did not stay to watch the performance of my fellow artistes.

Recently, for reasons known only to themselves, I was invited to address a conference of statisticians. I know nothing of statistics. Nevertheless I did not hesitate to point out to them that 73 per cent of statistics were simply invented. Nobody laughed.

I have spoken to groups of the old and groups of the young. I have spoken to a conference of people who operate buses. I have spoken to breakfast clubs and dinner clubs and investing clubs. I once addressed a gathering of stockbrokers (Is there a collective noun for stockbrokers? If not, could I suggest a drear?) and I took the opportunity to explain money to them. The dollar, I said, did not exist. It was merely a shared belief. If people stopped believing in it, the dollar would disappear like a burst balloon. The response of the stockbrokers was less forthright than that of the rugby league players, but it was identical in tone.

I am grateful to my speaking jobs for the money they've earned me, the glimpses they've given me into other people's lives, and the funny stories they've afforded me once the pain has worn off, but I remain puzzled by them.

If I turn down an invitation to speak, the inviter always asks whether I know someone else who can do the job. The implication is obvious. Rather than having sought me out for my unrivalled combination of wit and beauty, they came to me simply because they'd heard that I might be able to plug their gap. That gap is the speaker's gap and what puzzles me is that the speaker's gap exists. Why do people want speakers?

Most speeches are dull. People don't so much enjoy them as endure them. Think of the speeches you have heard at prize givings. Think of the votes of thanks, the sermons, the Queen at Christmas, the after-match formalities, the wedding stuff, the inaugurations, the formal welcomes, the keynote addresses (whatever keynote may mean), the motivational nonsense, the staff meetings.

And yet I know several people who make a living entirely from public speaking. There are bureaux from which you can hire speakers at preposterous expense. A large number of these speakers are known not for their speaking but for something else – for climbing mountains, say, or for playing netball. Playing netball is an admirable thing, as is climbing Mount Cook on one leg without oxygen and with a goat over each shoulder, but neither guarantees a good speech. Presuming that it does is like expecting an All Black to be able to repair the hard drive of your computer on the grounds that he's an All Black.

But there exists something in the psyche of our society that says an event is not an event unless it is consecrated by a speech. I don't know why.

I was once hired to address a school reunion. I had not attended that school. I knew no one at the reunion. I was hired only because the organisers felt that a speaker was needed. He wasn't. Most of the audience had not seen each other for anything up to fifty years. They had plenty to talk about. But the occasion required that they shut up and listen to me. I did not stay on my feet for long.

A while later I found myself at the urinal. Two elderly men of battered appearance appeared beside me but did not notice me.

'That was a great evening,' said one.

'Yeah,' said the other, 'apart from that bastard who spoke.'

'Hear hear,' I said softly to the porcelain, and toddled home with my cheque.

Money matters

Welcome to Money Matters, a column so occasional that this is the first one, in which our experts answer your financial questions.

Q. I have been specially selected to attend a seminar on how to become ridiculously rich by working from home for only half an hour a month. The seminar lasts a whole day and costs only $895 plus GST. There has to be a catch in it, but I just can't see one. Can you? Perceptive of Invercargill.

A. If you can't, Perce, nor can we.

Q. Can Money Matters explain the difference between tax avoidance and tax evasion? I have not completed an income tax form for several years and am hoping that what I'm doing is the legal one. Name and Address Withheld, though it's not far from an airport just in case.

A. Good question, Mr and Mrs Withheld, and one we are often asked. Tax Avoidance means legally not paying tax. Tax Evasion means illegally not paying tax. Or it may be other way round. In order to qualify for the legal one, you have to have so much money that you wouldn't notice if you did pay tax on it.

Q. Eager of Matamata asks, how do I get lots of money without doing anything to deserve it?

A. Well, Eager, you'd be amazed how often we are asked this question, and here at Money Matters we don't mince words. Unlike a lot of financial advisers who hide behind jargon in order to avoid telling the harsh truth, we make a point of monitoring the key economic drivers, especially in the derivative and Forex markets, which allows us to factor in the current position of commodities futures in order to give you the straight answers.

Q. Can I put my American Express bill on my Visa? Hopeful of Motukarara.

A. Sounds a cracking wheeze to us.

Q. Why, asks Sceptical of Whangarei, do the banks call their investment funds 'products'?

A. Good question, Scep. The dictionary defines a product as the sum arrived at by multiplying one figure (figure A) by another figure (B) to arrive at a third figure (X). In the case of bank products, A is the sum of money you invest over, say, five years, and X is the lump sum you receive at the end of that period. In our experience with the principal retail banks, the figure B is rarely higher than 1.

Q. We have heard that the Sage of Omaha is very good for predicting the movement of investment markets, but my greengrocer has never heard of it. Would seaweed do instead? Herb of Timaru.

A. Seaweed has been shown to predict economic results more

accurately than most analysts.

Q. Two years ago I bought a lounge suite from a department store on the promise of no interest and no repayments for two years. Now, out of the blue, the store has started asking for money. I have explained that it is inconvenient for me to pay them anything right now, but they are becoming quite surly. Should I go to the ombudsman? Also, am I correct in believing that the numerous beer stains on the sofa will work to my advantage? Hurt Feelings of Auckland.

A. Given the flattening yield curve in the bond market and the softening of the outlook for first-ranked debentures, yes.

Q. I see that company directors get paid a lot for not doing much. I have written to several large companies and offered to become a director, but the few replies I have received have been brief and discouraging. In consequence I have decided to found my own company and appoint myself chairman. What salary should I start myself at, do you think? Rising Entrepreneur of Winton.

A. Whatever you think. You'll go far.

Q. I have just started my own company, and appointed myself chairman, but I am struggling to make meaningful use of the word 'leverage'. As a result I feel that I lack business credibility going forward. Can you help? Hopelessly Simple of Tuatapere.

A. We certainly can, Hopelessly. Treat the word leverage in the same way as you treat 'meaningful' and 'going forward'. If you really want to impress, you might also like to consider using the phrase 'the business cycle'.

Q. I have heard that there is such a thing as a debt market. I would be very interested in selling some of my debts. What's the going rate? Or is it just another game that only the big boys are allowed to play, with the honest worker missing out yet again? If so, please explain what financial people mean when they refer to the gearing of debt. Is it possible for me to gear mine? I would be keen to engage reverse. Alternatively, I have noticed that the big boys retire debt. How old does a debt have to be before you can retire it? I've got several elderly ones. Indebted of Auckland.

A. None of these processes is as easy as it looks, Indebted, unless you acquire some meaningful leverage going forward in the business cycle.

I want some of that

Before July 1980, I'd have said anaphylaxis was a Greek novelist. Then I got stung by a wasp. It almost proved to be the last time I got stung by anything.

The wasp got me on the back of the neck. By the time I reached hospital I looked like the elephant man on one of his worse mornings. My neck was wider than my shoulders. They had to turn me sideways to get me through the door. Breathing was proving an absorbing challenge.

The doctor injected adrenaline directly into my vein. To say it was exciting is like saying that the war in Iraq was misguided. Intravenous adrenaline is almost worth being stung for.

A few years later I met a girl in France whose father was an allergenist. He offered me a free course of desensitisation. The process involved injecting me with a minute quantity of wasp venom and then holding me captive in the surgery. Monsieur le Médecin's ostensible purpose was to ensure I didn't suffer an adverse reaction. His actual purpose was to deliver an hour-long illustrated lecture on why England and the English sucked. I never went back. I preferred, on balance, to run the risk of meeting the Greek novelist again.

For the subsequent quarter of a century wasps have left me alone, but I have been reminded of them recently because I am tempted to start keeping bees. I am not allergic to bees.

I don't know very much about beekeeping but I suspect that there's not much keeping involved. If the bees decide to leave I can't see myself shooing them back into the hive. I also doubt the dogs' ability to muster bees. (To be frank I doubt my dogs' ability to muster anything except an appetite, though Jessie used to be a dab hand at shunting chooks around the garden to no purpose.)

I'm not certain what attracts me to beekeeping. It certainly isn't the uniform. I don't see much joy in togging up as if for a moon landing and then clambering up the hill in the middle of the summer carrying a sort of fire extinguisher in order to pacify and rob several thousand armed insects. The reward, of course, comes in the form of honey but for one thing it takes an awful lot of bees an awful lot of time to make not an awful lot of honey, and for another thing I don't like honey. And even if I did I could get a jar of it for five bucks from the supermarket without dressing up like Neil Armstrong.

No, if I kept bees it would be in the same way as I keep dogs, goats, a cat and tadpoles (and whitebait until the cat got them). It would be non-productive, costly indeed (though tadpoles are admittedly inexpensive to feed) and my rewards would be only pleasure and interest. And animals are easier to live with than people.

Since conceiving this interest, I have read a little about bees. They are seriously odd. Everything centres on the queen who is selected young like the Dalai Lama and fattened on royal jelly. She then buzzes out of the hive once, mates and returns to lay eggs. On a good day she can pump out 3000. But she doesn't have to raise the family. All that stuff's done by the workers who are female but infertile. Workers nurse larvae, clean the hive, guard the hive, collect nectar, make honey, make wax, store the honey behind the wax, clean the lavatories and die young.

Bloke bees meanwhile lie back with their heads on their hands, dabbling in poetry, sipping cocktails and once in a while getting up, yawning, stretching, and toddling over to the queen to see if she fancies a bit of rumpety pumpety. It all sounds admirable. It's also ruthless. When the mating season's over so is life for the blokes. They're starved and driven from the hive whereupon they're not going to get taken in out of sympathy by any old drones' home. A short life but a merry one.

But apparently it is wrong to think of bees as individuals. The hive is rather a single organism like a human body and we should think of individual bees in the same way as we think of body parts. So, just as we don't consider kidneys to be independent entities that resent their lousy job and dream of promotion, so we shouldn't fret about individual bees. They are part of the whole, like kidneys, like cells, and the whole is everything. Bees don't mind dying.

All of which I find intriguing and I think I'd like to have some of that around the place, though how you go about starting is something I haven't learned. But I have learned that bees are often attacked and killed by wasps. I think bees and I could get on.

Rugby Exposé. Young Players in Drinking Shock. Former Great Lashes out against Booze Culture. Never-before-published Liver X-rays of Top Players – Your Own Super Bumper Souvenir Lift-out. Exclusive.

'We drank so much we got drunk.' With that one short sentence former rugby star Joe 'Fairy-cake' Bennett has fired an arrow into the heart of the Rugby Football Union. In his first searing autobiography, due in bookstores just as soon as the pre-publication hype reaches its zenith, Bennett lifts the lid on the steamy debauchery that underlay the glossy image of the fabled Queens' College Second XV of the late 1970s.

No reputations have been spared. Of coach Mick 'Teddy Bear' Raw, Bennett writes, 'He acted as though it was his job to tell us how to play. He liked drinking beer.' Of notorious prop forward Steve 'Biscuits' Allison, 'He was fat. He liked drinking beer.' Of winger Paul 'Plastic' Denvir, 'He got so cold on the wing he played in two shirts. He liked drinking beer.'

When we rang these three legends of the game, their wives said that the possibility of legal action over Bennett's book had not been ruled out, and their husbands were in conference right this minute with advisers at the Pig and Whistle Legal Bureau.

Acting on a tip-off from a publicity release we tracked down 'Fairy-cake' Bennett to the media centre at Hypit Forrall Itsworth, the public relations company that handles many of the top players. Bennett was trying to hide from the attention behind a bank of microphones.

Speaking slowly and pausing frequently with obvious emotion at the thought of the sales this would generate, Bennett declared that he was a reluctant whistle-blower. 'But how can a man just stand by and allow his career in rugby to end without exploiting it financially?' he said, his sincerity evident to all. 'More importantly, how can a man stand by in silence when he sees young men going to the pub, drinking in groups and enjoying themselves?' he added, his sincerity evident to nobody.

'I remember,' continued Bennett, 'my very first training session at Queens'. It ended in a drunken game of "Bunnies" in the college bar. I didn't even know the rules. Did coach "Teddy Bear" Raw explain those rules to me? No, he did not. He presided over my humiliation and loss of trousers. He was a ruthless dictator who just didn't care. I was shocked and appalled. And when I finally made it into the Queens' second XV I was even more shocked and appalled. There was beer in the dressing room! And did Teddy Bear do anything about it? Yes, he did. He drank most of it. I was even more shocked and appalled. I lived in perpetual shock and appalledness. Even at that early stage I knew it would be my duty to speak out fearlessly thirty years later. I no longer care how it will affect my selection chances. Someone has to tell the truth before my name is forgotten and a book becomes impossible. How else is the general public ever going to know the truth behind the notorious Quattro Staggioni Pizza and Catapult Incident of '77, or what actually happened during the French tour of '78, and in particular the Sock Full of Rice Pudding Scandal? All I want to do is set the record straight. And if the truth hurts, well, let Teddy Bear write his own memoir. The rugby book market is a bottomless well.'

But Bennett insisted that his first duty was to the game he loves. 'Rugby is full of grand traditions and I have always striven to maintain them,' he said, 'and the tell-all terminal autobiography is a tradition that I happen to care deeply about. I am not ashamed. Writing the book was a huge emotional release.'

'The words just came pouring out of me in an unstoppable torrent,' confirmed A. Wraith, Bennett's ghost writer. 'I felt every bit as strongly as Bennett did about the size of the publisher's advance. Sure we had to pad the book out with tedious stuff about Fairy-cake's childhood, his failure to make any rep teams, his utter inability to tackle, but there was enough good oil on his former team-mates for me to know it was a winner. Rugby and revelations spell success in the Christmas market. Fairy-cake and I had a moral duty to our bank accounts.'

Sponsors were said to be considering their options in the light of Bennett's book. 'We simply do not condone drinking in any way, shape or form, and in particular we refuse to countenance any association between college rugby and drunkenness. It's just not what we're about,' said a spokesperson for long-term sponsor of Queens' rugby, Horizontal Breweries. 'Has Bennett no sense of conventional commercial hypocrisy?'

Ruck 'em All and Pass the Grog is published this week by Findan, Angle and Floggit at $34.99, and will be forgotten next week by everybody.

On making a bed

Oh dear, I've been walloped by envy. I want to start again. Because of a bed.

Beds don't matter much. This winter I spent two months overseas and hired a different bed for each of sixty nights. They shared a horizontal quality, more or less, but nothing else. Some sagged. Some were stiff with sheets and blankets, some wildly European with duvets, many rich with evidence of previous occupants detectable by nose and eye, or even touch. But I slept fine in all of them.

I've never bought a bed. My first house came with two. I've slept in one with dogs for eighteen years, and those among my guests who have not cared to join us have occupied the other. They've not complained and nor have I, except in warmer summers, and then it's simply been a case of making with the aerosol and all the fleas have died. Fear and guilt and even what I thought was love have stopped me sleeping, but never once the bed. In short, my bed has served.

But recently the bed has wilted. The thing has lost its buoyancy, the will to boost the dogs and me against the pull of the earth. In winter that's just dandy. It makes a warm and snug cocoon for us to wallow in. But I fear the heat of summer.

And so I went to buy a bed. The bed shop offered beds of every kind except for waterbeds which once were everywhere but suddenly in 1996 or thereabouts they all collectively and simultaneously sprang a leak and shrivelled into landfill. I don't know why.

Nor do I know the collective noun for beds – a slumbrousness, perhaps – but here for me in this enormous showroom it was a bewilderment of beds. So many, so various, and yet so similar.

An assistant sashayed over.

'I want a bed,' I said.

'What sort of bed?' he said.

'A nice one.'

The assistant led me through a string of questions designed to find the bang right bed for me and me alone. Among other things he asked me the position I slept in.

'Lying down,' I said.

'Ha ha,' he said.

'Ha ha,' I said, although I didn't get the joke.

'Show me,' he said, which seemed a little intimate, but I lay on the nearest bed, a sumptuousness of foam and no doubt hidden science, set within a bedroom's worth of chests of drawers with tilting mirrors, bedside tables and a dinky reading light. And there in front of the assistant I curled into the foetal shape that I've adopted every sober night since Kennedy was shot, and closed my eyes.

'Right,' he said. 'I think the bed you need is…'

'This one,' I said, for I was bored already and the bed felt fine. 'How much?'

He named a sum.

'No, no,' I said, 'I don't want all the beds in the shop. How much for this bed?'

He repeated the sum.

'Golly,' I said. 'And how much is it without the bedroom's worth of incidental furniture?'

He repeated the sum. 'Golly,' I said, 'but at least the mattress is comfortable.'

'The mattress is extra,' he said.

'Golly,' I said again. When I've found the aptest word I'm not afraid of repetition. 'To sum up, then, for something close to $3000 I get a bed without a mattress.'

'You're onto it,' he said.

I left. I'd made a resolution. I would make a bed. It can't be hard – a frame, some slats, a bolt or two, then slap a mattress on the top and get your head down. I said as much to a friend in the pub, a part-time cabinet-maker. 'It's harder than you think,' he said, 'but if you like I'll make you one.'

'How much?' I said.

The price he named was good. 'A deal,' I said.

He delivered it this morning. The thing's a wonder. It's solid as Mount Cook. The headboard gleams, its ancient heartwood rimu grain a maze of loveliness. The slats are firm as a bank. The whole's as square as Don Brash. I knew as we assembled it that I could never have made it.

And I was seized, racked, filled, crammed, with envy and admiration and regret. Envy of the skill of making. Admiration for the skill of making. And regret that I would never learn to make.

To make is good. Instead of spending time on hateful work to earn the dosh to buy the things we want, we should work less and save the dosh by making. How good and fresh and personal and true to make the furniture you use. How right and satisfying.

I want, right now, to start again, at school, and this time I will work in Harry Barker's woodwork class instead of playing pranks. But that's a dream. Too late, old boy. I'll write these words and take regret to bed.

Equopp tots

Baa baa, black sheep, have you any E?
Yes sir, yes sir, first hit's free.

That, according to my computer, is an ad once used by the 'Partnership for a Drug-Free America' to persuade parents that their children knew more about drugs than the parents might think. But it was swiftly taken off the air for fear that kids might learn the parody nursery rhyme before they learned the original.

The original has been around for 700 years. Apparently it began as an ironic commentary on wool tax. The 'master', who got one third of the proceeds from wool, was the king, the 'dame', who got another third, was my old friend the Catholic church, and 'the little boy who lived down the lane' was the farmer who owned the sheep and did all the work. Not much different today, I suppose, although at least the power of the church has waned.

But people still have to believe in something, and the people in charge of nursery schools in Oxfordshire, England are no exception. They believe in Equal Opportunities which for the sake of brevity I shall call Equopp. Stuart Chamberlain, manager of the Sure Start Centre in Oxford, is a fan of Equopp. 'We've taken the Equopp approach to everything we do,' he boasts.

'Everything we do' includes 'Baa Baa Black Sheep'. And sure enough when the nursery rhyme was tested on the Equopp Offensivenessometer, the needle whizzed into the red zone and Equopp warning sirens went off. 'Baa Baa Black Sheep' made opportunities unequal.

Why? Because, says caring Mr Chamberlain, 'no one should feel pointed out because of their race, gender or anything else'.

Well, I'm sure he didn't mean the anything else. I'm sure he didn't mean that no child should be praised and therefore pointed out for painting a pretty picture, or for helping teacher mop up urine, or for declining a free hit of E from the friendly neighbourhood pusher. No, what Mr Chamberlain meant, I presume, was that no child should be judged for something over which they have no control, such as the colour of their skin or, and this one puzzles me a bit, their sex – though of course Mr Chamberlain is so up-to-date squeamish that he doesn't say sex. He says gender, which is wrong, but let that pass. Here the obvious worry is skin colour. So it's bye-bye, black sheep, hello, and I am not making this up, rainbow sheep.

It is also, I presume, bye-bye to Snow White. And it is seriously and incontrovertibly bye-bye to the seven dwarves. Height is every bit as much a source of discrimination as skin colour. So let's hear it for Snow Rainbow and Her Seven Assistants of Average Stature. At the same time, by a rational extension of this Equopp principle, a case could be made for banning the words brown, yellow, boy, girl, blond, tall, short, fat, pretty, clever and astonishingly stupid nursery school manager.

Mr Chamberlain's attitude invites many questions, not all of them polite, but I shall concern myself with only two. First, does 'Baa Baa Black Sheep' 'point out' black children? If the tots of Oxfordshire were to chant, as they will never do, this nursery rhyme, would all the white tots instantly look round, alight on a black tot and point a jeering finger? Call me a jaded old realist but I suspect not. Lots of research shows that kiddies aren't born racist. They have to be taught to be so. And Mr Chamberlain may even be doing some of that teaching.

My second question is whether black children feel that they are being pointed out by 'Baa Baa Black Sheep'? Again, I suspect not. Indeed I would be willing to bet a tonne of black pudding to a slice of white bread that there have been no complaints from black parents or black children about 'Baa Baa Black Sheep'. I am confident that any of them who have thought about it will have noticed that the noun to which the adjective black is applied is 'sheep'. And they may also have noticed that out there in the world of reality where things are things, one of the many things that the evolutionary lord has planted on the surface of the globe alongside the black people and the white people, the black rhinos and the white rhinos, the blackboards and the whiteboards, is a black sheep. A black sheep is not a black child.

So why is Mr Chamberlain getting upset on behalf of people who are not getting upset? I'll tell you. It is because of a human habit that has done every bit as much harm in this world as warmongering. It is the urge to do good. Doing good makes people feel gooey inside, but it springs from exactly the same desire as warmongering. It springs from the desire to feel superior.

Furthermore, and quite predictably, the nursery school authorities of Oxfordshire are so intent on doing good that they have paid no attention to scansion. The word black has one syllable. Rainbow has two. Thus at a stroke the ancient human joy gained from rhythm is discarded in favour of the equally ancient human joy gained from feeling superior. Poetry nil, patronising nonsense one.

Baa Baa Rainbow Sheep have you any bull?
Yes sir, yes sir, a kindergartenful.

It's enough to drive children to drugs.

Goats beat flowers

Ever been seduced by goats? I recommend it. It's the very best form of gardening.

In the time before goats I did not have a distinguished gardening history. I bought my first house twenty years ago and it came with 900 square metres of New Zealand. Those metres were steep and infertile – like Queenstown without the tourists. Nevertheless I thought it might be good to garden, so I planted a small feijoa tree. It remained a small feijoa tree for a while and then it became a small feijoa tree without leaves and then it became a small feijoa stick. I didn't argue. There is little point in arguing with the dead.

I gave up arguing with the grass too. The grass wanted to be two foot tall. I wanted it to be an inch tall. The argument went on for a whole summer. When I broke my third mower I realised that inch-tall grass was mere conformity. It was the suit and tie of gardening. And 2-foot tall grass hid the feijoa stick nicely.

Five years later I sold my steep 900 square metres with grass and feijoa stick and bought 600 steeper square metres with grass, a kowhai tree, some agapanthus and a lot of weeds. Fancying a weed-free garden, but not wanting to weed, I added chooks. I got a weed-free garden. I also got a grass-free garden. The chooks didn't eat the kowhai because they couldn't reach it and they didn't eat the agapanthus because it's like eating a glossy magazine, but they reduced the remaining 550 square metres to bare earth with craters. It looked like the Somme circa 1917. I didn't argue. Indeed I didn't mind. In the summer the chooks bathed in the dust and dropped eggs in the craters. In the winter they hid under the house. The agapanthus thrived without intervention from me.

And then last year I found goats. They came with a house and a steep hectare of land. I didn't like the house much but I did like the hectare and I loved the goats. I bought the house in ten minutes. When I rang up a friend to boast, she asked how many bedrooms it had. I said I didn't know but it did have two goats.

'Goats?' she said.

I tried to convey the wonder of it all. 'Yes, goats,' I said.

'Goats stink,' she said.

'They're a long way from the house,' I said.

But goats don't stink. They're lovely. They inhabit a pair of paddocks at the top of my hectare. I go up at all hours to feed them, to stare into their smoky eyes, to stroke their soft angora pelts. They respond by nuzzling my palm, and headbutting each other. At present I am building them a crude house to shelter them from the winter to come. I like building crude stuff. It is manly and satisfying and it offers me the excuse to buy tools. I have bought a chainsaw.

And there I think is the nub of the matter. I am a bloke. I may not be a manly bloke. My hands are soft urban hands. My profession is words. I drink fancy foreign lagers. I have been likened to Julian Clary. I didn't mind being likened to Julian Clary. But I remain a bloke. And for a bloke, or at least for this bloke, building beats gardening and goats beat flowers.

Goats also eat flowers. Between me and the goats stands a rock garden. I bought the house in winter. In spring I watched with wonder as flowers sprouted in the rock garden. Pretty flowers, expensive flowers, a few of which I could name but most of which I couldn't.

I didn't argue. Indeed I didn't mind. When people came round they said, 'What a pretty rock garden.'

'Yes,' I said, 'thank you.'

But among the expensive flowers there sprouted other flowers, most of which were yellow, all of which were weeds. They were stronger than the expensive flowers. I found them neither more nor less attractive. Nor did the goats.

The goats like to rub against the gate at the foot of their paddock. They rub with vigour and an obvious physical pleasure. I've never seen a flower yet that displays obvious physical pleasure. One day the chain that holds the gate snapped. The goats discovered freedom. By the time the dogs and I discovered the goats they had also discovered the rock garden. Like me the goats did not distinguish between expensive flowers and free ones. I didn't argue. Indeed, I didn't mind.

In the deep midsummer

Sing heigh ho and recreational sex, it's that time of the year again. The time when firkin-gutted old men delve into the wardrobe that smells of dandruff and disappointment, to haul out the crimson uniform made of genuine 100 per cent nylonette. A quick sniff of the fabric confirms that a year's neglect has bleached the more bitter overnotes from the armpits, then on it slips, over the wrinkled dugs and the swollen belly and the shrivelled loins and the varicose veins and the gleaming shinbones. Add a hat like a windsock and half a metre or so of guaranteed flame-retardant draylon beard and it's yo ho ho time all over again. For the children, you understand.

It just wouldn't do to disappoint the little sweethearts who, with their rubber limbs, unblemished skin and self-whitening teeth, are innocence made flesh, their loving little souls beaming like the rising sun from their XXOS eye-sockets, and all of them gaga for a bit of wonder.

And for the best yo ho ho this year, why not take them to the profoundly traditional and spiritual Carols by Candlelight, held in the Wellington sports stadium? The stadium is named after a bank whose employees have risen in protest against instructions from the boardroom to press crippling quantities of Asian credit on already impoverished mums and dads so that they can shower Xbox consoles on their offspring to educate them in the necessary ways of the world, but who cares about all that? 'Tis the season to be jolly in the spirit of Shoppingmas, when all is joy and Chinese-made tinsel. The novelty bait at this year's Carols by Candlelight is that Santa is going to arrive by flying fox, just as he did all those years ago in Bethlehem. 'Oh, please, Mummy, can we go, can we, please, please, pretty please?'

Twenty thousand roll up. But they have to wait. Santa will be the climax. First comes the spiritual fumbling, the undressing of Christmas, as it were, before the final eruption. Carols. Ah lovely. Good King Wenceslas trudging through the snow (that we haven't got), 'Deck the Halls with Boughs of Holly' (that we also haven't got), the plangency of 'Silent Night' – ah Bach, ah beauty – and then, 'Look Mummy, look up there. Is it Baby Jesus? Is it, oh-my-God, Santa?'

But it isn't Baby Jesus. It isn't Santa. It's better than that. Up on the platform high above all mortal beings, up there where hope and dreams dwell, a mere spit from the portals of heaven itself, stand the Immortals, the true spiritual entities of today, the Cartoon Characters. Behold in the nimbus of the follow-spot, the blessed family of the Flintstones, and the angel that is called Shrek. Down the long wire they come, unthinkably real, and the children are sore with spiritual delight. 'Oh, Mummy, that was *wonderful*.'

A pause, a drum-roll and suddenly it's Santa time. On the lofty ramparts he stands, poised to swoop, his harness barely visible beneath the swathe of synthetics. Yo ho ho and here he comes, descending from the skies, the ancient god of acquisition coming to earth. 'Oh look, Mummy, look, oh look, oh …dear.' For something has happened.

Santa's stuck. The god is dangling, his descent from on high impeded, stalled, his gleaming shinbones kicking weakly in the spotlight of misfortune, his costume ruched about his hips, his progress halted a hundred feet up in the sky. It's his beard. His beard is caught in a pulley. The flame-retardant draylon simply refuses to give. And before the fire brigade can scramble, the kids are scrambling, gathering right underneath jolly old Santa as his face turns the colour of his costume.

The innocents, the darlings, the tinies, the future of the teeming globe, tomorrow's busy economic units, are milling beneath Santa by the hundred, peering up and pointing at the suspended deity, who is silhouetted against the early evening sky as in a medieval painting of the ascension. The kiddies have an unimpeded view of the divine undergarments, Chinese-made and plugged by that alternative Pantheon, the All Blacks.

Santa is effectively lynched, swinging impotent above the crowd of innocence, a gift from the sky that the sky has had second thoughts about, and the kiddies' dismay is so intense that they squeal and laugh and point at his discomfiture and every last one of them hauls out his photo-enabled cellular telephone bought with the credit urged on his heavily-mortgaged parents by the very foreign bank in whose temple they have congregated, and snaps the godhead in distress. The children are ecstatic with schadenfreude. Oh, the sweeties.

The time will come, of course, when they will learn to mask their delight in the misfortune of others, when they will sit in front of the pornography that is the television news and learn to tut and to pretend to be appalled, but for now they are radiant with honesty and make no effort to dissemble their delight.

Ah, Christmas. May you all have a merry one.

Tribal stamps

'Awesome,' he says, 'that's the only word for it. Awesome.' His grin seems to stretch twice round his head. The stadium is on its feet. The noise is tumultuous and it is his. Years of dedication, of unstinting self-denial, of monomaniac commitment, have reached their thunderous apogee. His team-mates have just stripped to the waist and done a haka, a haka for him alone. He is the garlanded hero. 'Kiwi, Kiwi,' bellows the crowd.

'I'd like to dedicate this medal,' he says into the microphone, 'to every philatelist in New Zealand.' He lifts the medal from his chest and holds it beside his face where it swings and glints in the stadium lights. 'It isn't mine, it's yours.' The crowd roars with tribal approval of this modesty, this generosity.

The winner strides off to high-five those members of the crowd who have managed to fight their way to the rail beside the arena. Cut to the studio.

'Well,' says the beaming anchorman, 'a great night for New Zealand, and scenes that will be etched into the memory of every one of us. We hardly dared to hope for a stamp-collecting medal at these games, but Gavin has astonished and delighted us all. To be honest, I'm close to tears. We've done it. We'll take a short commercial break while I fetch a handkerchief, and when we come back I hope we'll have an interview with the man of the moment.'

Breakfast cereal cascades from a packet into a gleaming porcelain bowl decorated with the New Zealand flag and scenes of sheep and rugby. The backing theme is stirring, anthemic. A freckled child digs a giant spoon into the bowl, morphs into a muscled Adonis in a leotard and sprints away towards a long shot of Mount Taranaki. On the mountain's snowy summit stands a stamp album that opens to emit a blinding golden glow, like a sunrise, majestic, entrancing. As the athlete runs towards the glow, the music rises to a climax that stirs hairs on every scrotum in the land. The athlete raises his arms in an orgasm of triumph and is absorbed by gold. It's a long ad. The cereal manufacturer is the Official Energy Supplier to the New Zealand Commonwealth Games Team. When it's over, there's time only for a stilted and unconvincing pharmacist to plug wart cream before we're back in the studio.

A dust of make-up has taken some of the glow from the anchorman's forehead but not from his grin. 'In case any of you have just switched on, the great news is that we've picked up a gold in the Standing Freestyle Philately. And the man of the moment, still basking in his victory, is with me now in the studio. So, Gavin, congratulations from the whole country. How does it feel?'

'I'm struggling to believe it right now. I'm frightened I'll wake up and discover it was all a dream.'

'Ha ha. Well, let me tell you it was a dream come true for all of us. Talk us through the final moments. At what stage did you know you'd won?'

'It was the Mounting and Alignment section of Weimar Deutsche-post low-denomination Kaisers that clinched it. I got in the zone and then I knew.'

'It must have felt great.'

The athlete grins. 'We've been doing a lot of work on it at the Academy.'

'The Academy?'

'The Philately and Numismatics High Performance Academy. Without it I don't think I'd even be at the games, let alone on the podium. So I'd like to take this opportunity to thank not only my family, my supporters and my dedicated Academy coaches, but also the government who had the vision to create the Academy in the first place. Ten years ago they sensed that sporting achievement had the capacity to lift a nation by proxy, and they also had the vision to see that sport was simply a competitive activity, and that any activity could be rendered competitive. So, following the international Kiwi triumphs in lawn bowls, which unbelievably had once been seen as a mere recreation for the elderly, then indoor bowls, which unbelievably had once been seen as a recreation for the seriously elderly, and the prone pistol, which unbelievably had once been seen as just someone lying down and keeping very still, and darts, which unbelievably had once been seen as a pastime for drinkers with no conversation, and poker, which unbelievably had once been seen as the ruin of many a vainglorious man, the government took the lead in establishing an élite corps of full-time professional philatelists and numismatists. Tonight's the pay-off. And I urge all stamp-collecting athletes of whatever age to follow your dream and to believe and to go on believing, and one day, like me, you could find yourself standing before your team-mates as they perform the special stamp-collecting haka with its unique gestures of album-opening and tweezer-use, and like me you could know that four million Kiwis from Cape Reinga to the Bluff were making the floorboards ring in time with them. Oh, I can't go on. Forgive me if I weep.'

'Viewers of New Zealand,' says the anchor down the barrel of the camera, 'let us weep.'

Mister Muster

Failure is better than success. Failure is funny and it teaches you stuff. It also inoculates you against hubris, the pride that the gods enjoy pumping into your heart before they introduce the banana skin.

In general, then, I am a fan of failure. But today I have to report a success, a success that has pumped me as full as a blimp with hubris. The event was the summer muster.

The summer muster is a staple of televisual farming. It appears on *Country Calendar* and on Speight's ads, which are more or less the same thing. Farmers prepare for the muster by donning Drizabones, applying make-up for that seriously weathered look, mounting horses, surrounding themselves with dogs, and riding slowly up the winding track towards the snowline, saddle-bags crammed with tins of beans and the air thick with guitar music. Then the director shouts cut, the music stops, the farmers dismount, the horses go back to the props department and everyone gets into a Toyota Hilux.

My muster involved neither horses nor Hiluxes. It involved two sheep, two goats, one small paddock and one large labrador. What made it a triumph was that they said it couldn't be done.

By they I mean he. He was a Banks Peninsula farmer with whom I played cricket last week. Actually he was watching the cricket rather than playing, because he had been temporarily disabled. A calf had kicked him in the knee for reasons that the farmer did not elaborate.

I explained my mustering plans to him in the hope of receiving tips. I received discouragement. After ten minutes of discouragement I was tempted to drive to Banks Peninsula and buy the calf a beer.

It was the labrador that provoked the farmer's particular scorn. Labs were, he said, the very worst dogs with sheep. He told me cheerfully how many labs he had had to shoot. They totalled one, but one was ample to alarm me.

I readily admit that Baz is not a sheep dog. He would like to be a sheep dog, I suspect, but only in the manner that a lion would like to be a wildebeest dog.

'Forget it, Joe,' said the farmer in summary. 'Get a proper dog and someone who knows what they're doing.'

I told him that I had got someone who knew what she was doing, a warm-hearted woman who keeps a few sheep, and shears them herself. She is approaching seventy years of age but I didn't tell the farmer that.

Averil arrived at my station on Tuesday morning with two sets of shearing blades and an infectious confidence that I would have liked to be infected by. We climbed to my steep little paddock. Averil admired the pen in the corner, and pretended to admire the race that I had constructed out of waratahs and chicken wire. Baz the lab and I had tested the race that morning by trying to herd the chooks down it. Baz enjoyed the procedure enormously but didn't quite cotton onto its purpose. The chooks cottoned onto it immediately. I consoled myself with the thought that sheep can't fly.

The sheep and goats had taken refuge in a distant corner of the paddock. Averil waited by the race while Baz and I went up the hill to muster. We took with us, respectively, a vigorously wagging tail and a vigorously beating heart.

The sheep stared at the dog. The goats stared at the dog. The dog stared back. 'No,' I said, and he didn't. 'Stay,' I said, and he did. I approached the stock. They skittered down the hill. The dog did not move. 'Good dog,' I said in a tone of voice that I hoped did not betray my astonishment.

'Come,' I said, and he came. 'Sit,' I said, and he sat. The stock skittered further down the hill. I skittered after them. Every few yards I summoned Baz and repositioned him. It was like repeatedly shifting a roadblock with teeth. That the stock moved away from the roadblock did not surprise me. That the roadblock did not move towards the stock, did.

We crept ever closer to the chicken-wire race. The stock made a bid for liberty up the hill. 'Stay,' I said and the roadblock stayed. So did the stock. I held my breath. The stock moved towards the pen. Man, woman and dog closed in. And the goats and the sheep went meekly into the pen. 'Well, bugger me,' I said. The hills were ringing with the gods' applause.

Five minutes later I was learning how to shear and Baz was fast asleep under a pine tree.

Shearing proved a breeze. We whistled through it. When the dog woke up an hour later we were already onto the second sheep.

Another forty minutes and Baz didn't even bother to stand as the goats and the shorn sheep raced past him and out of the pen. The fleeces were as rich and sweet and dense as pride. I carried them down the hill like booty, my labrador sheep dog happy at my heels, my heart as fat as a cauliflower, my mind already riffling through the phone book in search of a Banks Peninsula number, and my eyes scanning the horizon for the banana skin to come.

May I join you?

Dear Ecowarrior,

I hope I've got the right bloke. I Googled Ecowarrior, but all it came up with was the address of some fortified kibbutz growing organic carrots on the Gaza Strip. The Ecowarrior I want is the one dodging Jap harpoons in an inflatable somewhere near Antarctica, and if that's you, carry on reading. If not, please forward.

I haven't got much to say, though that's probably just as well since I doubt that you've got time for correspondence, what with 30-foot waves, an oceanload of whales to care for, and a fleet of Jap factory-ships full of blood-spattered 'scientists' with their feet up waiting for the Mitsubishi sonar to latch onto anything over 20 feet long whereupon a bony Jap finger presses the red button and it's sayonara, Mr Minke, long live the emperor and sake all round.

I saw you on the telly the other night and all I want to say is that I want to join you. I realise there may not be a vacancy right now, but surely it's only a matter of time before one of you collects a harpoon amidships. As you probably know, they're rigged to explode about three seconds after contact so there won't be much anyone can do. (You're also, by the way, going to struggle to bring back enough pieces to justify the full Lamb & Hayward environmentally sustainable interment option with biodegradable casket, which is a pity because everyone back home would be only too keen to get out there for a bit of green ceremonial and a good blub.)

But anyway, I want you to know that I'm just itching to leap into the boots of any fallen comrade. The reasons are pretty obvious. Here in suburbus drearius there's a distinct shortage of fun, not to mention warfare. For the first time in history, peace is officially top of the pops. Every bleeding-heart secondary school in the land devotes more hours a week to peace studies than to the three Rs combined, though quite what there is to study about peace, I've no idea.

The upshot of the universal official wetness is that we young blokes can't find anything much to satisfy our giant adrenal glands and our genetically programmed urge to be chest-beatingly combative. There's drag-racing, of course, and rugby, both of which are all right in their way, and then there are the PlayStation gore-fests manufactured by the same toothy boffins you're up against right now, but it's all pretty tame stuff. And in comparison with the fun you're having, it's like a Tuesday night in Tuatapere.

I expect you know and care as little about minke whales as I do, but you couldn't have picked a better banner to charge into battle under. Everyone rallies to the whale. It's become a symbol of our cringing guilt at being global top dog, and boy do we like feeling guilty. So pretty well everybody in these parts is right in there behind you, and you, of course, can feel you're on the side of the angels, which is always a help when it comes to swinging the lead. You're a bit like those self-immolating fanatics in the desert with their fatwah against the imperial Yankee devil. They know they've got Allah and half the Middle East behind them, and you know you've got the whole of the wet West. It must feel delicious.

I don't know if you've heard, and I'm not sure that you're going to believe me if you haven't, but back here the eco-lobby has been urging the woman with the bad teeth to send you a frigate. Brilliant, isn't it? Those same vegetarians who five years ago were squealing that every dollar spent on frigates was a dollar spent on war games for the boys, games that reflected an archaic misapprehension of the current mood of the globe where at last we were beginning to realise that we were all in this together and that only by pulling on the same rope while singing from the same hymn sheet could we save the rainforest, the whales, the ice-caps, the bicycle and David Attenborough and prevent the planet frying to a crisp, suddenly those selfsame people are screaming for a frigate with the safety catch off and a Jap in the crosshairs. Lovely.

Mention of the rainforest brings me to another bit of news that may not have reached you. Apparently some German test-tube wallah has discovered that public enemy number one in the battle against global warming isn't BP, General Motors or Dick Cheney. Believe it or not, it's the tree. Apparently every little *Pittosporum beneficus* is pumping out greenhouse gases and winding the global thermostat another notch towards boiling point. The eco-lobby, having always based its case on man-nasty/nature-nice science, is understandably struggling to put a decent spin on this one.

But all that's by the by. I'm confident you don't give a monkey's whether whales or the human race keep going twenty more years or twenty million, and nor do I. You're just out there for a bit of warfare, a sense of heroism for an apparently virtuous cause and above all to get the good juices flowing. And I want to join you. If you've got time between whales to scribble a note I'll be forever in your debt.

Yours with glandular enthusiasm,

Joe

In the trolley

He was standing at the bar and looking glum. I thought I'd cheer him up.

'Do you ever wonder?' I said, though even as I said it I doubted that he did. Like all of us who'd gathered in the pub that Christmas Eve, he was intent on drink. The only wonderment he might be feeling was whether he'd be served before he died of thirst. The barman was a dolt. He dished out drinks with all the vigour of a sloth on Prozac. And he approached the electronic till as if it were a suitcase unattended at an airport. Each time he touched a key, he looked as though he thought it might go bang.

And yet the barman should have been at ease with all things technological, for he was young and very up to date. He'd dyed his crew-cut purple, and from his brow and cheeks and lips and nose there hung about a pound of polished chrome.

I began again. 'Do you ever wonder,' I repeated, 'when you approach the checkout at a supermarket, whether what you've gathered in your trolley, that tin of Oak baked beans, that pack of ham on special, that jar of Rose's breakfast marmalade, in short that random aggregation of consumer goods that you have chosen from the crowded multicoloured shouting shelves…'

'A Benedictine,' said the man. He didn't say those words to me, but to the barman who to everyone's surprise had managed to fulfil an order, operate the till, accept some money and, with suitable delay for computation, return the customer a sum approximating to the proper change.

'A what?' the barman said.

'A Benedictine,' said the man again. The way in which he said it was as up to date as facial piercing. He spoke with rising intonation, as if it were a question, as if he wasn't confident the syllables of Benedictine meant anything at all. It's a style of speech that's popular with the young. A friend of mine once labelled it the imbecilic interrogative.

The barman looked predictably bemused but slowly turned and scanned the mirrored shelves behind the bar as if they were his first sight of a foreign city. And I resumed my cheery questioning.

'I'm sure you will agree,' I said, 'that every trolleyload of goods reveals a lot about the way the trolley-pusher lives. The contents form a physical biography, an intimate and honest tale of needs and wants and attitudes. Indeed a glance at any trolley tells you more than you could learn from talking to the trolley-pusher. It tells you how much cash he's got and who he lives with and his social class. If studied thoughtfully it even tells you how he sees himself, or, as modern jargon puts it, his degree of self-esteem. In short, each trolleyful of stuff is fascinating, a private thing, like underwear revealed in public. In years to come I do believe the checkout will be curtained off for privacy. But all that's by the by. The thing I really want to know is whether you have ever wondered…'

'Is this the stuff?' the barman said. He held a bottle out. Across the label was a single word. That word was Benedictine. I wanted to congratulate the chromium-laden barman in terms so overdone that even he would sniff a hint of irony, but I held back. And so did gloomy Benedictine-man. He checked the label carefully.

'Yes,' he said, 'that's it.' The barman turned again to start the tricky job of pouring out a glass. I thought I'd better hurry and complete my question.

'So,' I said, 'and here's the nub, have you ever wondered at the checkout whether your trolleyload of stuff, selected from the vast array of products on display to fill our bellies, clean our houses, banish pests and keep our pets and us alive, your four bananas, say, and Fresh'n'Fruity yoghurt, your can of oven-spray and string of pre-cooked sausages, is unique?' I paused a moment, hoping.

The man said nothing, He just watched the barman who was continuing to make things happen with the speed of glaciation. Then finally the barman turned and laid a glass upon the bar. A note changed hands. I did not have long.

'Whether,' I continued, as though I'd merely stalled to draw a little breath, 'whether anyone else, anywhere in the world, in the whole and unrestricted history of supermarket shopping, had ever assembled precisely – and I mean *precisely* – the same collection of goods as you? And if not, if your trolleyful is indeed unique and probably never to be repeated, don't you get a teensy-weensy thrill from that, a sense that somehow it confirms the drunken randomness of things, the fierce absurdity and giant variety of life?'

The man received his change. He looked at it, then slowly turned to look at me. 'No,' he said.

'Okay,' I said. 'Happy Christmas.'

He left behind a little sticky ring of Benedictine on the bar.

The Grid of Seduction

My mother telephoned at Christmas and I learned that she does Sudoku. My mother is eighty-two.

I do Sudoku as well. I am forty-eight. My dogs don't do Sudoku. My dogs are dogs.

My mother says that she does Sudoku because she enjoys it but also because the exercise of thinking helps to fend off Alzheimer's. I enjoy Sudoku too, but I don't feel the need to fend off Alzheimer's because I smoke. Apparently few smokers go gaga. Either there is something in cigarette smoke that keeps the marbles in place or else cigarettes kill you before the marbles can wander.

I do Sudoku over breakfast while the dogs chew bones. A bone engrosses a dog but a bowl of Hubbard's Yours Fruitfully doesn't engross me. I need brain fodder at the same time. Sudoku is the purest brain fodder. It is ruthlessly logical.

The logical patterns are inflexible. If a, then b, and if b, then c. There is no guesswork. In the harder puzzles the chain of logic extends: if a then b, if b then c, if c then d, and if d, what was a again? For what makes the hard puzzles hard is that they test the limits of the short-term memory, the number of mental balls you can keep simultaneously in the air.

It is similar to telephone numbers. If you tell someone a six-digit number they will be able to recite it back to you. Seven digits and they possibly won't. Nine, and they definitely won't.

Whenever I do a Sudoku puzzle I am reminded of fourth-form algebra. Our teacher was Dim Jim who had eyebrows like caterpillars. His Bible was Hall's *Algebra*. It was a hard-bound book the colour of withered orange-peel and it consisted mainly of columns of exercises. There would be, say, fifty quadratic equations of increasing difficulty. Dim Jim would demonstrate the method required to solve a quadratic, a demonstration that involved much caterpillar activity, then he would set us to work our way down the column of examples while he sat at the desk and gave the caterpillars a break. I liked the whole business. I liked the moment when I grasped how the method worked, I liked applying the method, and I liked the neat way it solved the problem.

No one ever asked Dim Jim what quadratic equations were good for and if they had, Dim Jim would have just waggled the caterpillars a bit and told us to get on with it or else. For quadratics, as far as I can tell, have no purpose. I have never met a quadratic equation since the fourth form and now that more than half my life is over I can confidently predict that I won't. But I can still recall the pleasure of solving them.

They were a perfect, vacuum-sealed world, complete unto itself, where problems had solutions and where when something was done it was done. The rest of school was not like that. It was an indeterminate mess. Hence the pleasure of algebra, which was not a mess, and also of Sudoku. But hence also the addiction.

There is a moment in a Sudoku puzzle when you crack it. Though only half the grid may be complete you know that what lies ahead will be straightforward. Two minutes later the grid is full and that's that.

I read recently that the only phrase Hitler knew in any foreign language was 'Vous etes mon prisonnier'. That is exactly how I feel when I complete a Sudoku puzzle. It is what I've been striving to achieve for the last half-hour. It ought to be a good moment. But it isn't a good moment. It's a bad moment. What was engrossing throughout a bowl of Yours Fruitfully, a mug of thick coffee and three cigarettes is suddenly dead and devoid of interest. I am post intellectual orgasm.

And just as post actual orgasm I wonder what all the excitement was about and whether the expensive and protracted game was worth the brief flaming of the candle, so it is with Sudoku. My brain is now bereft of a precise and achievable task. I am faced with the mess of the day ahead, the day of inconclusive imprecisions, of shades of grey. Unless, of course, there's another Sudoku puzzle available, its grid temptingly incomplete, offering me the pleasure of its perfect logical sanctuary. I start again on the trudge up the hill to another pointless and disappointing intellectual spasm of relief.

Sudoku is a pastime. It is formulated to please our fat brains. It is adapted to gratify us as the world isn't. My dogs don't need pastimes. They finish their bones and then, if there's nothing going on, they sleep.

The values of Minscum

Calloo callay, oh frabjous day, the world is coming right. Two minutes past the yardarm this morning and I poured myself a snorter, sat down with the paper and discovered that the police are going to be issued with Tasers. Tasers are stun guns.

Henceforth, drop litter in the street and Constable Bigfoot will reach for his holster. 'Hold it right there,' he'll bellow. If you make a run for it, whoompha. Three hundred thousand volts will leave you squirming on the pavement begging for less.

Magnificent news, of course, but that was far from all. I turned the page and, well, let the article speak for itself. 'The Ministry of Education will introduce new values to the national curriculum…As part of a ministry curriculum review, a comprehensive list of values to be taught in schools has been put together… including honesty, respect and responsibility….Ministry Senior Curriculum Manager Mary Chamberlain said teachers wanted more advice on what values to teach.'

Call me a crusty old conservative but my heart leapt. There's nothing it likes more than a few old-fashioned values. It was the work of a moment for me to seize my snorter glass and hie me down to the local secondary school, locate its eaves and drop from them, applying my glass to the wall and my ear to the glass. And this is what I heard.

A previously valueless teacher was addressing a class of eagerly attentive fourteen-year-olds.

'Good morning, class of eagerly attentive fourteen-year-olds,' he said.

'Good morning, Mr Previously Valueless Teacher,' they chorused as one, that one being the winsome Samantha Plainbody. The remainder of the class were busy at the back being dishonest, disrespectful and irresponsible with an assortment of educational paraphernalia.

'We have a visitor this morning, children. Her name is Miss Ministry Senior Curriculum Manager. Say good morning.'

'Good morning, Miss Ministry Senior Curriculum Manager,' said Samantha.

'Thank you for your warm welcome,' said Miss Ministry Senior Curriculum Manager. 'I know my title's a bit of a mouthful. Please call me Minscum. That's what my friends call me, and I just know we're going to be friends.'

Deftly raising an umbrella to ward off the rain of expletives, condoms, syringes and other educational paraphernalia, Minscum continued undeterred, aware that the little darlings could hardly be blamed, having all been raised in a moral vacuum into which she was about to release the life-giving air of

'Values, children. I'm here to talk to you about values.'

'What's them, Miss?'

'That's a really good question, er…'

'Weedpusher, Miss.'

'Weedpusher, thank you very much for your contribution. Values are things that you've been deprived of by your dysfunctional upbringing. But now the Ministry of Education is going to rectify the deficiency with an ongoing integrated values programme initiative which in half an hour a week will undo all the harm of your formative years and rewire your skulls entirely so that you'll become sound members of the community and pay your taxes cheerfully, thus enabling the Ministry of Education to continue such vital work as paying Waikato University to survey teachers and parents in order to find out the value they place on values. Isn't that exciting? Anyway, children, values are what used to be called morals.'

'What's them, Miss?'

'That's another really good question, er… Runtface, and if you just put your beer down for a second I'll explain. Values are the things you used to go to Sunday school to fail to learn. They are concerned with right and wrong.'

'What's them, Miss?'

'Goodness, what a lot of excellent questions you're coming up with, children. You are a very bright class. How sad your intelligence is unmatched by your values. Still that's what I'm here for, to lead you through the moral maze and to release you from the torture of relativism.'

'What's them, Miss?'

'I think that's enough of your really good questions just for the moment, children. Let me ask you a question instead. Who's heard of honesty?'

'Me, Miss, me, Miss, me, Miss,' rose a mighty chorus.

'Excellent,' exclaimed Minscum. 'I can see I underestimated you.'

'We was lying, Miss.'

'Oh dear, lying's terribly irresponsible and disrespectful.'

'What's them, Miss?'

'Well, now, irresponsible means not accepting that there are consequences to your actions and disrespectful means…' but Minscum never managed to explain what disrespectful means because the previously moderate flow of missiles swelled to a torrent that rent the cloth of her ministry umbrella. Minscum fled the room, acquiring as she went a collection of minor bruises that she would eventually show off under Any Other Business at the next meeting of the Values

Curriculum Development Subcommittee.

'There,' she said, when she and the Previously Valueless Teacher had gained the sanctuary of the corridor. 'I think, if I may use a sporting metaphor, I've done the hard yards. I'll leave the squidgy ones to you.'

'Thank you very much, Ministry Senior Curriculum Manager,' said the Previously Valueless Teacher. 'I'm sure everything will be just fine now. Enjoy your return flight to Wellington and keep up the good work.'

'Oh, and this may come in useful,' said Minscum, handing the Previously Valueless Teacher a Taser.

Dead good

I don't know what you do on a Sunday morning, and I'm not going to ask, Sunday morning being a time of privacy and self-indulgence, but I do know what I do. At the crack of lunchtime, I leap from my virginal bachelor bed linen, and race the dogs down the drive. The dogs invariably reach the *Sunday Star Times* before I do, but I bribe it from them with a hunk or two of osseous beef. Then I wipe the saliva from the paper's wrapper, find the edge of the cellophane in well under fifteen minutes, unfurl the many fat pages of delight and throw most of them away. I throw away the hard news stuff, the soft porn stuff, the lifestyle stuff, the celebrity stuff, the car stuff, the sport stuff, the travel stuff – oh, especially the travel stuff – but I retain and settle down with the business stuff. My reason is simple. I just love a laugh. And Sunday morning, though, as I have said, a time of privacy and self-indulgence, can, with the attendant silence of commercial inactivity, descend too easily into lassitude or even gloom. But give me the business section and any hint of gloom lifts in seconds. It's a laugh a paragraph.

For starters, there's fun to be had from the stories. I especially enjoy the prognostications of economists, those witch doctors of our times. They flick through the entrails of Treasury figures, thumb the textbooks of theory, mutter a little necromantic jargon – the yield curve, the business cycle, global demand pressures – and deliver themselves of a prediction: a hard landing, a soft landing, a dead-cat bounce, an appreciation, a depreciation, a tightening market, a commodity boom, or any of the other set phrases that are as meaningless as the clatter of urine against stainless steel. Like urine they disappear with a gurgle and are forgotten.

But what matters is that the prediction has been made. The expert has employed his expertise and a ritual has been performed. It reassures. The economists' predictions, never tested, never returned to, exist solely to give a sense of a world under control, a thing understood. They are indistinguishable from astrology.

But the predictions of economists are merely an aperitif to my main delight in the business pages. I turn rapidly past the bespectacled grins of chief executives, the lottery results of the stock market, and financial advice from the guru who has clearly never made much dosh himself or he wouldn't be reduced to writing financial advice, and I turn to the appointments section, the advertisements for jobs.

Down I settle with my bowl of cereal, my vat of coffee and my fresh-peeled packet of fags, for an hour or more of delight. Oh, how I chuckle. I chuckle so hard that the dogs look up from their engrossing bones, their deep brown eyes awash with wonder. Poor things, in their world of efficient transmission of opinion through barks and growls and tails and hackles, they can never know the joy of mangled language.

I like to play a little game with myself. I like to read the text of an ad without first reading its headline, and see if I can guess what job it's advertising. And though I consider myself an aficionado of job ads, I am still often flummoxed. Consider, for example, this one, which I puzzled over, reread and admired. Oh golly gosh, did I admire.

'Here is your chance to join a unique industry and make a difference. You will have proven customer management experience and have the ability to build strong relationships with existing clients and attract new business. Exceptional communication skills are required with a focus on diversity. You will also have the ability to provide a quality service with attention to detail. This is an opportunity to join an innovative business providing a highly valued service in the community.'

To illustrate the comedy of job ads I could quote from a thousand of them, pumped out by recruitment agencies whose whole sad lives are devoted to this art, but I don't need to. For here, in this single brief example, is their art in little.

Here are the clusters of pompous abstract nouns that they so love to use to give the illusion of substance. 'Customer management experience' will serve to represent all such clusters. It means nothing.

Here too are are uplift phrases that give a little fizz of zeitgeist warmth. 'Focus on diversity' is a cracker, as is 'make a difference'. The prospective candidate feels warm and flattered and excited.

Here are buzzwords – unique, innovative, valued – mere noises of suggestion, but noises that infuse the text with a sense of being contemporary. And here above all is verbal inflation, reflected for all time by the pseudo-scientific 'communication skills', a phrase now so pervasive that a generation has arisen round us who can use it without collapsing into fits of giggles.

Oh, I do love my Sunday mornings. The text I've quoted is advertising a job at the Counties Manukau cemetery and crematorium.

That's entertainment

Rita was a disappointment, but didn't you just love Katrina? I couldn't get enough of it. If this is global warming, bring it on.

It's one thing seeing the impoverished suffer. We get that all the time and frankly I barely bother to watch. Another flood in Bangladesh? Who cares? Lots of little heads bobbing around the Ganges Delta like so many corks, where's the fun in that? The undeveloped world's got a lot to learn about the zoom button and the radio mike. I mean you just don't get the full effect if the only shots are taken from the one Bangladesh Air Force chopper at 10,000 feet by a nervous amateur toting a thirty-year-old ex-NBC videocam. It's like televising footy in Christchurch from the top of Mount Cook. There's just no passion, and no passion means no entertainment.

Third world disasters also lack novelty. You can more or less set your watch by the annual Bangladesh flood. And as for the Iraqi insurgents, aren't they hopeless? (By the way, what about that word 'insurgents'? Bet the White House boys riffled through the *Webster's* for weeks before they came up with that one, because even they knew you couldn't call the madmen 'terrorists' or 'rebels' when they were obviously just standing up to the Yankee invaders who'd waltzed onto foreign soil with their night-vision glasses and their No.1 haircuts and without so much as a by-your-leave. I mean, shift the perspective an inch or two and the only word available is patriots.) But as I was saying, if the insurgents want me to take more interest in what they're up to, frankly they've got to come up with something more original than suicide bombing. It's been done. And suicide bombings don't even offer an after-match manhunt with old Bushbaby going puce and screaming 'Wanted Dead or Alive', because they've already got the culprit in the form of 500 charred morsels scattered over a 2-mile radius. When will these people understand that a sophisticated Western television audience is a fickle thing that's never more than about ten seconds from a state of catatonic boredom?

If the insurgents (I'm still chuckling) can't find anything more original than the old dynamite waistcoat, they could at least give the media a bit of warning about when and where. I mean if there was actual footage of some nutcase pedalling into the marketplace on an antique Raleigh, then pulling the ripcord and suddenly hey, what marketplace, what wouldn't the networks pay for that? They'd bung it on the front end of every bulletin in the Western world, along with some deep-voiced fibmeister intoning that the following scenes might disturb some viewers, which is a surefire way of pushing the ratings through the ceiling, and then they'd show the best bits half a dozen times in super slo-mo. But no. All we get is the rubble twenty minutes later and a bit of ritual wailing, and frankly when you've seen that once you've seen it as often as you want to and it's time for the remote and *Coro Street*. Which is no way to win hearts and minds.

So the entire Third World from the Gaza Strip to the battling Congo has got a lot to learn about making the most of its disasters and the people they should learn from are the Yanks. They're the industry leaders. Take Katrina. They knew they were onto something nice and early, with lovely pics of stuff swirling round the Caribbean like a Technicolor catherine wheel with a bruise-coloured bit in the middle that just screamed of good footage to come. It was like the build-up to a test match. Then came all those shots of the lily-livered lardy-bums on the run in their overheated SUVs, while the poor or mad nailed plywood over their windows and prayed to the good Lord. I love that stuff in particular, the way they keep saying they've put their trust in the Lord when the Big Boy's intentions are emphatically laid out on the weather map in the most vivid colours that Microsoft can come up with.

Being a rich place, of course, the States is swimming in cheap Japanese handycams, most of them gathering dust in the basement, but one whiff of a wandering hurricane and up they pop like daffs in spring. So you get blanket amateur coverage – roofs flying, refineries exploding, corpses floating down the main street in Walmart jeans, all in close-up.

And then there are the reporters, all heading in exactly the opposite direction to the locals and vying with each other for the Foolhardiness Cup. What drives them is the hope that they might get hero status and a gong for best footage or most ravaged three-days-beard look, while what drives you and me back home in Safetyville is the hope of seeing one of them picked up by the twister live on camera and found three weeks later on a roof in Wisconsin, microphone in hand and vulture at the ribcage. It hasn't happened yet, but hope's a winner for keeping a bloke stretched like a violin string and glued to the sofa where the advertisers need us.

Old Uncle Sam still leads the world in entertainment.

On biffing a sock

I could write about the rise of fundamentalism or the decline of literacy, but I would have no effect on either. And besides I am preoccupied with a sock.

According to P.J. O'Rourke, a bloke's apartment needs to be cleaned once a girlfriend. After that, says the good O'Rourke, 'she can get to know the real you'. Not having a girlfriend, I can always be the real me. The dogs care as little as I do how deeply I sink into squalor. But I do still have to do laundry.

I lob soiled clothes into a basket in the bedroom. I have placed the basket in a corner so as to maximise the chance of catching rebounds, but underpants are aerodynamically dysfunctional, balled socks bounce erratically and shirts tend to drape the rim of the basket like corpses over a battlement.

Still, the flung clothes gather in more or less the same place, and when the heap grows large enough to hide the basket, or when it is emitting a fragrance suggesting the early stages of fermentation, or when a month is up, or when I have run out of habitable underpants, whichever is the soonest, I lug the basket to the laundry. The basket is a sexist basket. It is designed with a concavity on one side expressly to rest on a jutting hip. Being a bloke I do not have a jutting hip.

The basket implies that women still do most of the world's laundry. The basket is bang right. Women have always been more devoted than blokes to cleanliness. I remember once leaning on a bridge over a Spanish river watching a scene as old as humanity. Down below me peasant women were cleaning clothes by smashing them against rocks, and singing as they did so. If I had been one of those women, I wouldn't have been singing. Indeed if I had been one of those women, my family would have gone smelly.

But fortunately I live in an advanced capitalist economy that has fostered the entrepreneurial Messrs Fisher and Paykel. A month's worth of washing requires me to press two buttons. Three cigarettes and a chapter of O'Rourke later, I am faced with a choice. I can either tip the washed clothes into the tumble drier, whose artificially heated air will cost me money, exploit the world's diminishing resources of energy and melt another molecule or two of the polar ice-cap. Or else I can return the clothes to the sexist basket and carry them into God's own back yard, singing a peasant-woman song as I go and filling my lungs with healing draughts of the freshest autumn air. Then I can peg the clothes to the line where they will dry for free beneath an azure sky while seagulls lilt above them on the breeze.

When the tumble drier has done its stuff, I haul the clean clothes back into the hip-hugging basket and return to the bedroom. I toss the underpants and handkerchiefs into a drawer, and sort the socks into pairs before tossing them into a different drawer. I used to hang trousers and shirts in the wardrobe but have recently realised this was one step too many in the laundry cycle. I now lay shirts and trousers directly on the bedroom floor. That done, I feel good. I have a sense of completion, of neatness, of preparedness to take on the world afresh. I have order. Or I would have were it not for a sock.

Some while ago I completed my laundry cycle as described only to be left with a single blue sock in the laundry basket. Confident that I would gather up its mate when next I did the laundry round, I left the clean sock in the bottom of the basket.

A month or so later I laundered again and was again left with the solitary blue sock. Though my faith had diminished somewhat I once again left it in the basket.

I have now washed that sock half a dozen times. It is a very clean fly in the ointment of order. So today I went looking for its mate.

I checked in the washing machine and in the tumble drier. Nothing. I checked down the side of the washing machine and down the side of the tumble drier. Two handkerchiefs and a flannel. No sock. Back in my bedroom I drew the curtains for the first time in years. Sunlight flooded in and revealed no sock. I crawled under the bed where the giant dust balls live. I even flipped the beanbags that the dogs sleep on. Several coins, half a biscuit and no sock.

Today is bin day and I have made a decision. I have just thrown out the sock. By doing so I have salved a tiny irritation, solved a tiny problem, and established a jot of order in a vast chaotic world. Which is more of a difference than I will ever make to the rise of fundamentalism or the decline of literacy.

Go tell it to the Stones

Philosophy's booming. Everyone's at it including the Rolling Stones. There was a picture of them in the paper, all grinning like chimps at the announcement that they're about to start rolling again by going on tour and releasing a new album. The announcement coincided with Mick Jagger's sixty-second birthday, and there they all are, presumably in the communal room of their rest home. Only they're not wearing rest home clothes. They're wearing the sort of leather jackets and black T-shirts that I lusted after at the age of seventeen then outgrew at nineteen having discovered corduroy, tweed and literature.

By rights the Stones should be dead. They propagated an image of excess, fuelled by drugs and long-legged, walnut-brained women, Rolls-Royces in swimming pools, hotel rooms reduced to rubble, jeans of a testosterone-inhibiting tightness and a general disregard for their own well-being and the need to keep something in reserve for tomorrow. For the Stones there would be no tomorrow.

Well tomorrow's arrived and the Stones are in it, all of them, looking a bit like prunes perhaps but well-maintained prunes with full complements of limbs, organs and even, to judge by the photo in the paper, teeth. Their bank balances are crammed, they don't need bus passes, they're still wearing jeans and they seem happy. It just isn't fair. There should by rights be some sort of reward for those of us who heeded the warnings and didn't go wild and did stay sober and industrious and watched what we ate and maintained regular hours and made do and said ah well never mind and put something aside for a rainy day. If we waited, the world would dish up a slow revenge on the Stones and reward us for our decency and obedience. Time would grind the Stones to crusher dust, and we would tut and feign sympathy while inwardly gloating and muttering that you reap what you sow and what goes around comes around and the wages of sin are death. But the wages of sin appear to have been wealth, fame, jeans, women and joy. The whirligig of time has failed to bring in its revenges. Jagger looks better at sixty-two than I do at forty-eight.

And perhaps the Stones have sensed that something strange has happened because they've suddenly got philosophy. Their new album is called *A Bigger Bang*, reflecting, apparently, 'a new-found fascination with scientific theories governing the origin of the universe'. The Stones are interested in how it all began. Or at least they purport to be. They have promised that their album will be a collection of 'hard-hitting' (which means loud), 'high-powered' (which means loud) 'rock and blues songs' (which means songs in which you can't make out the lyrics.) And even if you can make out the lyrics, going by previous songs of theirs, you won't be rewarded with much in the way of philosophical insights.

So where to for philosophy? It's obvious: Oxford, where they pay people to philosophise, people like Professor Richard Swinburne, who is apparently 'one of the world's leading philosophers of religion'. I haven't seen a photo of the Prof. Swinburne so I don't know if he goes in for Stones gear or corduroy gear or rest home gear or creaky philosopher tweed. Nor do I know if he's as young as a plum or withered like a prune. But I do know that he's nuts.

Prof. Swinburne has calculated, bless his little bag of lectures notes and his giant cranium like a bulb on a stick, that 'it is 97 per cent certain that God raised Jesus Christ from the dead.'

'This conclusion was reached,' reports the Melbourne *Age*, 'by a complex series of calculations. In simplified terms, it began with a single proposition: the probability was one in two that God exists. Next, if God exists, the probability was one in two that he became incarnate.' There's plenty more similar stuff in this complex series of calculations but I'm not going to quote it, because if those two fundamental propositions are sound philosophy then I'm Mick Jagger's toyboy.

On what logical principle did Professor Swinburne arrive at the notion that there's a 50 per cent chance that God exists? Presumably this professional thinker concluded that either God exists or he doesn't and what with there being no hard evidence either way then it must be fifty-fifty. Well now, what a cracker.

On that premise there's a fifty-fifty chance that astrology is good science, that at this very moment Elvis is cruising the aisles of a Walmart in upstate Tennessee, that Lyttelton is about to be attacked by giant moths and that tomorrow morning my arms and legs will drop off whereupon I shall be joined in bed by a giant panda and the band of the Grenadier Guards. Oh spare us.

Prof. Swinburne has written a book propounding his complex series of calculations in full. I haven't read it and I'm not going to, but I do think the Stones ought to set it to music. At least then we wouldn't be able to hear the words.

Beastly morning

You know it's going to be a cracking day when you slide out of bed and step into cat-sick. There wasn't enough cat-sick to make a noise when I trod on it, but there was enough for it to squidge up between the toes a bit.

Keeping the toes aloft, I Jake-the-Pegged to the kitchen, my nose wrinkled like a boxer dog's, and set the coffee-machine going. Then I Jake-the-Pegged to the bathroom. On the bathroom floor lay the scattered remains of a mouse: a tail, a ruby-coloured organ that looked like the heart and a firm little peanut that was once the mouse's stomach. The cat always discards these body parts. Perhaps she imagines they could make her sick. Well, she's got that wrong.

I hoisted my foot to the washbasin, which is not as simple an operation as it once was, and washed it in the hottest water I could stand, before throwing the mouse-parts from the bathroom window, and summoning the dogs to the bedroom where I tried to interest them in the cat-sick.

One dog in particular is a committed vomitivore. Indeed, being a labrador, he's a committed anything-carbon-basedivore. He took a promisingly adjacent sniff at the cat-sick, a sniff which I encouraged with yum-yum noises, but then he turned away. I did too. I was not going to clean up cat-sick until I had had coffee. Coffee led to a cigarette, the combination led to the lavatory, and then the tyranny of habit led me to take the dogs out.

The day's animal theme was not yet worked through. The lab caught a hedgehog which meekly submitted to being carried a mile or so to the car, where the dog released it, his duty to me, as he imagined it, done. I laid the hedgehog in the grass by the track to unfurl when it felt things were safe, and to begin the long trip home to its family with a story to tell and the nagging feeling in its belly that it wouldn't be believed.

Back home I had to fetch bones for the dogs from the freezer in the garage. Above the freezer is a swallows' nest. The nest sits on a book. Three months ago I wrote that the book was a Wilbur Smith, and I condemned the swallows' literary taste. I must now apologise. I had only got close enough to read the author's initials. The book is by William Styron, whom I have never read.

In December the swallows produced two offspring. On the day they left the nest, one of them flew straight out of the garage and into the house. It got trapped in the lounge. I reached it before the cat did, and carried it downstairs, its tiny frame pulsing in my softly closed fist, its head swivelling. I stood in the garage with the bird in my hand. The parents flew in, twittering as parents do. I opened my palm. The young swallow sat there. I could feel the grip of its tiny claws. I held my arm out. The parents swooped and fussed. The young one just watched them. Then it flew.

Since then I have seen it and its sibling repeatedly. They perch on a wire near my deck. As the summer has deepened I have watched the red feathers on their throats darken in colour. I have watched the swallows grow to be adroit murderers of insects, at which point the parents returned to child-rearing.

Of their second brood, only one hatched. For the last few days it has been sitting on the side of the nest preparing to fly.

When I opened the freezer it took fright and flapped its wings.

But it didn't fly. It just fell over the side of the nest and hung there upside down, its wings beating. I climbed onto the freezer, which is not as easy an operation as it once was.

A swallow's nest is a cup of mud, lined with feathers and guano. Feathers and guano had combined to form a sticky web, and the swallow's claw was trapped in it. The bird was effectively tethered. So once again I found myself lightly gripping the barrel of a young swallow's body. I reached into the nest and teased the claw from its tether. When it was free, the swallow sat for a few bewildered seconds on my palm, a few ounces of feather and flesh, ordering the world in its tiny mind. I had time to observe from the closest possible range the sleek low arrowhead of its frame, the tiny scissored dart of its beak, the faultlessness of its everything, so different from my lumbering middle-aged humanity. Then it flew. It was an instant master of aerobatics, dipping and swerving out through the garage door into the February sunshine, to be a swallow.

Refreshed, startled in a good and tiny way, I jumped heavily from the freezer, took bones up to the happy dogs, made more coffee, sat with it in the morning sun, reflected that it had been a pleasing start to the day, and went to clean up some cat-sick.

Up Apophthegm Mountain

I'm a sucker for the big notion, the sort of thing you find in the *Dictionary of Quotations*. Give me an apophthegm like 'Life can only be understood backwards; but it must be lived forwards' or 'If you want to make God laugh, tell him your plans' and I'll swallow it whole and commit it to memory. For the next few days I'll also regurgitate it whole to anyone who'll listen. And a fat lot of good it does either of us.

For the grand notion never quite fits. It rings true in principle but it omits the detail that constantly muddies the picture, the sort of detail to which I woke this morning. Drizzle masked the hills, my nose was full of snot and I had a hangover that turned my head into the mental equivalent of television static.

I should have spent the morning working but instead I spent it reading the collected letters of a dead and gloom-drenched poet who lived, it seems, in perpetual drizzle. The letters are crammed with small stuff, stuff that mattered at the time but doesn't matter now, stuff like recalcitrant lawnmowers and the price of chops. But then suddenly he startled me with a nugget of big stuff. 'If my life were a week,' he wrote at the age of forty-eight, 'then this would be Friday afternoon.'

The words pierced the hangover and the snot and sank deep into the pink. Ooh, I said, with a delicious shudder of dread, and I laid aside the book.

For I too am forty-eight. I too am on Friday afternoon, and there's only the weekend to go. Oh golly gosh.

As for the week so far, well, all the important stuff happened on Monday, and I've forgotten the lot. It's all gone, all the stuff that dictated every subsequent event has shrivelled into oblivion. When I look back on Monday I see only a vague and sunny land of lala. Tuesday morning was more of the same, but then round about lunchtime up rolled puberty and the weather turned thunderous. There followed an intense afternoon of rich and self-indulgent despair, the air charged with threat and thrill. Nothing since has matched it. Wednesday I spent more or less drunk. Thursday was industrious, energetic and stable. And then came Friday. Friday proved surprising.

Early on Friday I went back to the land where I was born and caught up with old friends from school and university, all of us the same age. And I found myself moving from crisis to crisis. It was as if a switch had been thrown in every male head. Stable Thursday lives had suddenly turned into Friday chaos. Husbands of model diligence had eloped with feather-headed long-legged secretaries. Sensible stockbrokers who slept in ironed pyjamas had fled to the hills to be potters. Everywhere I went, careers were in abeyance and marriages were rubble.

Rather than being a holiday visitor, I became an itinerant counsellor, a shoulder for weeping on, a receptacle for the big questions. I enjoyed every minute of it. And the synchronicity of it fascinated me. It was as if everyone had woken independently to the awareness that this was Friday morning, that the peak of the week had passed and that if a life was ever going to amount to anything it had better start amounting now. It was a subconscious crack of the existential whip.

I saw most of the wayward ones again this year. They'd mostly settled back down. Marriages were patched, careers resumed, and everyone had snuggled down to a Friday afternoon snooze amid the welter of small stuff.

And that in the end is what's wrong with the grand notion. It's all very well to clamber up Apophthegm Mountain to take in the big picture, the tour d'horizon, the great sweep of things, but all too soon it's time to return to the place we belong, down among the small stuff.

All other life forms have the instinctual good sense to stay down there the whole time. You don't see ants wandering off to become painters or to have a final fling before the loins wither into silence. They simply keep on keeping on.

My aged dog has just lain beside my chair. She's twelve years old, which in dog terms is Sunday lunchtime. She neither knows nor cares. Food and hunting and other dogs still interest her, and that will do. The big stuff is a uniquely human interest and it doesn't get us far.

'We are unsuited,' wrote the same gloom-laden poet whose letters I was reading, 'to the long perspectives open at each moment of our lives.' However neat and appealing it may seem, the grand notion, the vision of one's life as a week, is less significant in the end than a hangover, snot, drizzle, a recalcitrant lawnmower or the price of chops.